CW0621288

Being Aboriginal contains stories, observations and reminiscences from Aborigines who took part in radio programs made by Ros Bowden and Bill Bunbury for the ABC's Social History Unit.

It attempts to retain the character of the speaking voices which describe, often very powerfully, how some Aboriginal Australians experience life in white Australia.

Being Aboriginal

Comments, observations
and stories from
Aboriginal Australians

an
ABC
BOOK

*From the ABC Radio programs
by Ros Bowden and Bill Bunbury*

Published by ABC Books for the
AUSTRALIAN BROADCASTING CORPORATION
GPO Box 9994 Sydney NSW 2001

Copyright © Australian Broadcasting Corporation 1990

First published March 1990
Reprinted July 1992
Reprinted October 1993
Reprinted October 1997

All rights reserved. No part of this publication may be
reproduced, stored in a retrieval system or transmitted in any
form or by any means electronic, mechanical, photocopying,
recording or otherwise, without the prior written permission of
the Australian Broadcasting Corporation.

National Library of Australia
Cataloguing-in-Publication entry
Bowden, Ros.
  Being Aboriginal.

  ISBN 0 7333 0023 5.

  [1]. Aborigines, Australian—Biography. [2].
  Aborigines, Australian—Interviews. [3]. Aborigines,
  Australian—Social conditions. I. Bunbury, Bill. II.
  Title. III. Title: Being Aboriginal (Radio program).

305.899150922

Edited by Nina Riemer
Designed by Helen Semmler
Set in 10pt Schneidler by Midland Typesetters, Maryborough, Victoria
Printed and bound in Australia by Sands Print Group, Perth.

9 8 7 6 5 4

Contents

Being Aboriginal,

an Introduction by Ros Bowden

I first came across Aboriginal people when I was on a six month drive around Australia. Like most travellers I found my first images distressing. The Outback seemed to have groups of dusty drunks on every pub verandah, often accompanied by sounds of shrill arguments sprinkled monotonously with those famous Anglo Saxon four letter words.

The white people in the town explained it all away by suggesting that colour produced all this hopelessness, that black people were somehow naturally dim-witted and therefore could not manage their lives. Criticising these people for being drunk and hopeless while there were many equally badly behaved whites inside the pub did not provide any of the answers. Because I had spent a good deal of my childhood in South India and Sri Lanka where black people managed their lives perfectly adequately, I felt colour in itself could not explain things. A curiosity developed and I tried to understand what had led to the scene outside the pubs.

My reward has been constant challenges to my own perceptions. Almost every contact I have with Aboriginal people forces me to rethink the way I am conditioned to understand things. Accepted standards of cleanliness, the work ethic Europeans are all brought up with, our selfishness in capital accumulation for the benefit only of our close family, these all look pretty illogical when examined from a different angle. The road to the pub still stretches ahead.

Recording material for the ABC Social History series *Being Aboriginal* was part of this discovery process. I had contact with a variety of Aboriginal communities. The group involved with

Yipirinya School in Alice Springs were language speakers with a good part of their traditional culture woven into their lives. The people taken from their Aboriginal parents and 'raised to think white' were trying to make contact with their wider family and birthplace. This knowledge was their passport to acceptance in Aboriginal society. At CAAMA Radio in Alice Springs, American Country and Western songs were the vehicle for the characteristically Aboriginal custom of keeping in contact with relations living hundreds of miles away in the desert. Why not their own songs? I naively asked. Because, I was told, Aboriginal songs sometimes take six months to sing!

Many of the reasons for the scene outside the pub are now obvious to me. The solutions are less so. But as I listened to the customs and values of Aboriginal people explained to me so patiently and generously by all the groups I met, it made me wonder how long the white community can go on pretending not to hear and continuing to keep Aboriginal Australians waiting for justice.

Ros Bowden
ABC Social History Unit, Sydney 1990

A number of people were involved in each of my *Being Aboriginal* programs but in this book we have not attempted to identify each speaker separately. Those taking part, however, were: Coral, Lola, Joy, Robyn, Cherie and Kevin in 'Raised to Think White'; Essey Coffee, Les Darcy, Marlene Lord, Richard Sullivan and archival recording from the Australian Institute of Aboriginal Studies of Jimmy Barker in 'White Man Say We Have No History'; Freda Glynn, Ned Hargraves, Vince Forrester, Agnes Young and Isaac Yama, Emily Hayes and members of the

CAAMA staff in 'Language Is Our Lifeblood'; Eli Rubuntja, Theresa Alice, Rosie Ferber, Margaret Heffernan, Louise Raggett, Thomas Sevens, Anna Nora Rice and Dianne Ferber in 'Learning Two Ways'; Paddy Jerome, Bob Weatherall, Sam Watson, Don Davidson, Headley Johnson, Pat Murdoch and Roy Hopkins in 'The Spirit of Musgrave Park'.

Raised To Think White

'I was taken from my mother, my mother was taken from her mother, and my daughter was taken from me. *Link-up* isn't only about taking people home physically. Really, what *Link-Up*'s about is getting people home emotionally and in every way so that one day they can stand and say "I'm worth something" as an Aboriginal and as a person.'

. . . .

Nearly all Aboriginal families in Australia today will know of relatives who were removed as children and put into European care. They're the children the Aborigines refer to as 'taken'. Their place in their family is vacant but never abolished. Many of these people, now adults, are suffering a crisis of identity and want to rejoin their own people. But they've been raised to think white. To be accepted in Aboriginal society they need to learn a completely different set of rules.

Coral Edwards, Co-ordinator of Link-Up, *experienced all the difficulties herself when she went home to meet her Aboriginal family:*

'*Link-Up* started in 1980 with Peter Read and myself. It started because I went home to meet my family and it was after that, when we got back, I thought "Jeez, it's taken me this long to get home, there must be a lot of people around who are in the same boat" and that's when I put it to Peter. "How about we start something for people in my position, like me?" And that was how *Link-Up* started.

'We were rather naive at the time, thinking it would be so easy to start. We thought we'd only work with adults who had gone through Cootamundra or Kinsella [Homes] and we had no funding and had no idea where we'd get funding. We had no idea about the welfare system or where you found records or anything.'

But in spite of difficulties Link-Up *was established and people came for advice and help.*

'My mother was Aboriginal. The policy was to separate children, especially fair-skinned children, from the mothers as soon as possible. On my Certificate of Removal it said "Take the child from the association of Aborigines as she's a fair-skinned child." I think the rationale behind that was to raise me as white.'

. . . .

'I was adopted when I was, I think, about twenty weeks old to a white family in Sydney and that's where I grew up. They were a middle-class family and I grew up with one younger brother. We grew up on the Northern beaches of Sydney so it was a very middle-class suburb and there were no other Aboriginal people around that I knew of.'

. . . .

'I know for a fact that I was adopted when I was only a couple of months old. When I was younger I didn't want to have anything to do with Aborigines. I sort of thought of myself as being a white person. In fact, if ever I heard the word Aborigine I'd back away, so to speak, but that was when I was much younger, and then as I grew older and wiser I came to terms with it.'

. . . .

'I remember very vividly Central Railway Station as being a lot of activity going on. There was a Welfare Officer, a male Welfare Officer, and there was myself, my younger sister and my older sister and my brother. The male Welfare Officer was there to take my brother to the boys' home and I remember him crying to stay with us and the Welfare Officer dragging him away. That's been very vivid in my mind and I haven't forgotten. You know, that was quite a number of years ago, in 1951, when I was only four, and I don't have a memory as to why we were taken away.

'My next memory is of the Matron in the Home. I was told to go out back and wait for the other girls in the Home to come back from their walk. After that it sort of dawned on me, "Well, where's Mum?" She wasn't around any more.'

. . . .

'For quite a few years I grew up thinking I was an orphan, because all the other children used to have either one of their parents come in on visiting day, which was the first Saturday of every month—I'll never forget that—and I used to have no one so I sort of thought I was an orphan. Then I found out I had a mother. They also told me she was an alcoholic, she drank a lot, that she didn't want me and I had nowhere to go, but if I kept on playing up I would be sent to Cootamundra Girls' Home which was only for bad girls. I was running away, stealing. It came to a point where I'd shot through overnight and they took me up to the doctor to see if I was still a virgin, which I was, and then I was told the next day that I was Aboriginal and that I had mud in my veins and that my mother didn't want me—all in one day. And then I had to write out, I think it was 500 times, "God is Love".'

. . . .

Coral Edwards says she does a lot of talking and a lot of listening to the people who come to her:

'Listening more than talking—to find out how they're feeling

7

about themselves and how they feel about Aboriginals and what sort of misconceptions they've got, so that we can help them. A lot of Aboriginal people who come to us have been raised with a non-Aboriginal family and the only information they've got about Aboriginals is what they've got off the TV or the radio, which isn't always good—it's not a good image. So we do a lot of listening with them and a lot of crying with them. It's often the first time people have actually told things that they've never ever said before in their lives about things that have happened to them. It's a sort of an unburdening, if you like, to get rid of stuff and start afresh before they go on to the next step, which is meeting the family.'

. . . .

'Mum, foster mother, used to say things like "Oh, we'll take you to Redfern one day and we'll show you what your mother would have looked like." They'd say things like "She'll be sitting in the gutter drinking a flagon of wine", and all this sort of thing, and when you're a kid that's really scary. You get drummed into that kind of thinking that Aboriginal people are dirty and just wasted—that's the sort of ideas they put in you. When I went through school I just couldn't adapt really well to the other children because I was the only dark-coloured in the whole school. That's all I knew—I'm Aboriginal and I'm darker than anyone else, that's it.'

. . . .

'Comments were made—little things, like "Oh, she'll be going walkabout soon"—stereotype comments, and I used to wonder what the hell they were all about. I used to stand a certain way at the kitchen sink and I didn't realise that I was standing in what is now a stereotype Koori position. They'd come along and kick my knee so I'd fall and break dishes, so I'd have to go and write another thousand lines of a Bible verse—I was

8

a great one for Bible verses. But I just grew up with the feeling that being Aboriginal was bad.'

. . . .

'If I had been fairer it may have been a little easier—I don't know, but I felt like I was in limbo, like I wasn't one side of the fence or the other, that I was just stuck in the middle somewhere. We were constantly told to keep clean—you don't want to be dirty like the Aboriginals you see around. We were being raised to think white and act white and forget about anything that was Aboriginal.'

. . . .

'When I found out that I was Aboriginal, one of the biggest things that I had to start doing was looking really closely at all the things that I'd learned and the stereotypes. [I had to look] at things like being taught by white people—I don't just mean by that my family, I mean the school that I went to and the newspapers and just everything around me—the white culture that I grew up in. I had to start questioning all the things that I'd learned through growing up like that. I felt really frightened that I'd take all those judgments home with me and put them on my family, because they're wrong and an absolutely bad place to start from in trying to get to know your family. It's hard enough getting to know strangers anyway, let alone putting all these judgments and rubbish on them.'

. . . .

'I was 36 when I started to think that I was black, in my mind, because I had been working and living in white society for so many years. I've been discovering my Aboriginality since 1983 and there's no way that I will again think white.'

. . . .

'It took a long time to get over that thing of black not being a colour of your skin. I'd been taught to believe that to be black you have to have really dark skin. That's partly also why, growing up, it was harder for me to identify as Aboriginal, see myself as Aboriginal, because I thought that I didn't look Aboriginal enough to be Aboriginal. And all those things like, "You're so fair you can't be Aboriginal", and "What about the part of you that isn't Aboriginal?", and "What percentage of you is Aboriginal?"—all those questions were what I'd grown up with around me, so it is actually quite a long process, feeling that I could comfortably identify as black.'

· · · ·

'How many times have I heard said, "How can you really consider yourself an Aboriginal person when you had a white father, or if you've got white blood in you?" You cop it all the time from white Australians and I just say to them, "Look, you are what you are and I am what I am. I'm an Aboriginal person. What are you?" "I'm an Australian", they say. But what are they, really? What are white Australians? They're always questioning our identity and we always have to prove our Aboriginality, but when have white Australians ever proved their identity?'

· · · ·

Coral Edwards says it's hard to explain the need to find out about being Aboriginal.

'It just drives you. It takes over your whole life. You want to belong so much and you've got no base to start on, because if you start mixing with Aboriginal people the first thing they're going to say is, "What's your name and where do you come from?" And if you can't answer those two questions then you're gone. People can't connect you into the Aboriginal network because they don't know the name, or you don't know the name, so they sort of shut the door straight away. That's why it's really important for us to get to know what the natural name is, because as soon as we've got that name we can pick the area. For instance, my family name is Edwards and there are only three places in New South Wales where there are Edwards families. We talk about our country, our spot . . . Aboriginal families didn't move far from those areas. People say, "Edwards—where are you from? Are you from Bourke or from Balranald or Tingha?" and I say, "I'm a Tingha Edwards", and people just click you [in] because they know. One of the most common Aboriginal names probably would be Williams. Now, there are Williams not connected with each other, different Williams families from the North Coast, South Coast, out West, and Smith is another one and Johnson's another—we know Johnsons only come from certain areas. And so that's why it's really important for people to have that name so we can just click them in.

'If someone came to us and said their name was Williams, for instance, we would contact those areas and not just ring up. We don't ring up, we actually drive to that town and go and see the people, because it's just the right thing to do, and find an older person who'll remember. And the thing is with children being taken, people remember that. It's not something that's just forgotten, like yesterday's birthday party. They say, "Oh, yes, so-and-so had a child taken, you know, thirty years ago, or something like that, and she's married to, say, someone else now, but she was a Williams". People remember. You just don't forget something like a child being taken.

'People contact us through word of mouth. They ring through or write letters. A lot of welfare agencies—Aboriginal Child Care agencies, Youth & Community, any government offices, in fact, any enquiries at all now, they just put them on to us.'

'I found out I was Aboriginal when I was twenty-five through a fairly long process of firstly walking into the Aboriginal Legal Service in Redfern and going to see Jenny Munro and saying, "I think I'm Aboriginal. Can you help me?" And she did. She was great. She spent quite a few hours with me, talking and just making me feel that it was quite likely that I'm Aboriginal and that was a good thing to be.

'Then she wrote to Coral and *Link-Up* and they traced my mother, who was a white woman and who told them that my father's Aboriginal. Because I was adopted that all took about eighteen months.'

. . . .

'I wanted something fast, something that you could feel really quickly and there wasn't anything around. It seemed like such an effort.

'I was working at Newtown Social Security Office when I found out about *Link-Up* and I rang up and talked to Coral and she had a talk to me about what to expect and that she'd do her best. I think it was only about three months after that that she found my mother's name, and that for me was the biggest breakthrough out.'

. . . .

'We were just talking, just sitting there having a yarn, and Coral says, "Your mother's not Dora?" I said, "Yes", and she said, "You know, there's a lot of people looking for you". I said, "Oh, yeah, pigs might fly—who'd be bothered looking for me?" and she said "There's a whole lot of people in Cowra and they're all your cousins and your aunties" and she said "Yes, it's where your grandmother's buried". And that was marvellous, although it was very scary, too. Then Coral said, "Well, look, I'll take you home", and I liked the way she said "home". I was sort of thinking of a nest somewhere, and even then it took me a few weeks to decide whether I would go home or not. And that was horrendous. Oh, my God, I'll never forget it! You know, we were getting closer and closer to Cowra, tearing along the highway in a bloody white Commodore which reminded me of a welfare car, when I said to Coral, "Hey, come on, let me out here. You go on up to Cowra. The motel's already booked, so you go up and have a nice time and I'll just take a walk back to Nowra. No trouble, no trouble, I'll just go back. Bye-bye." Coral said, "Listen, Joy, we'll go to Cowra and book into the motel. If you don't want to go over to meet Val and your cousins you don't have to." We got to the motel, unpacked everything and then she said, "Now we've got to go and meet Val". And we drove up, but I was just sort of super-glued to the car seat and I started bawling my eyes out, and we went in and there was a whole lot of faces and names—I'm still learning names. And then she introduced me to Val and Val was just beautiful, just beautiful. She just said "G'day, love". She said "My grandmother and your grandmother were sisters." And I just flew to her. You know, we started crying and carrying on and, oh, it was marvellous. That was the first time I felt I *knew* who I was. It was like going into the womb and coming out born when I met Val, and it's been like that ever since, sort of growing up inside. Because inside I've got this family vacuum. I can't say, "Oh, when I was ten I did this with my cousin or I did that with my mother", but all that vacuum now is starting to be filled. And it's quite schizophrenic at times, too, because you've got this child growing up inside you and the *adult* you has to learn to let that child grow and it's very difficult.'

. . . .

'In a lot of people there's a stronger feeling of wanting to belong somewhere. That's not in all people, [though it] tends to grow in all of them, but at the initial meeting it's usually a curiosity to find out who you are, get your family history, and the rest follows after that, stronger feelings of belonging somewhere, and all the Aboriginal thing comes in as well.'

. . . .

'With relationships there are certain things in the Aboriginal society that you just don't do, and I'm learning those—what to do and what not to do. You can refuse a biscuit or a piece of bread or a piece of cake or something, but you never refuse a cup of tea. There are people that you go and see first, not a pecking order, but there are people you go and see first and people you spend a certain amount of time with. There are some that you can talk to about certain things and others who can talk about other things.'

. . . .

'Aboriginal families are so extended—that's the biggest thing I think, getting used to having heaps of people in the house, cousins, aunties, uncles. There might be ten living under the same roof. There might be a lot of them living on benefits. Some of them don't. A lot of them work some time. Always, if you've got money and your brother hasn't and he needs money to go down to the shop and get something, well, you'll just give him money and you'll give everyone money. If they need something they're very unmaterialistic. Money isn't an issue. It's surviving, you know, and we've all got to survive, so you give it away so everyone can survive.'

. . . .

'I was put through the hoops a couple of times. I made one horrendous mistake when I went back by myself the second time and Janie's fridge was empty. So, big magnanimous me, I decided to go out and do a whole lot of shopping and spent about $80 to $90 on groceries and filled up the fridge. That was in the morning. In the late afternoon nearly all the food was gone and I said, "Jane, look, all those bloody kids are running around eating this food that I bought for you. There's only one loaf of bread left." Then I opened the fridge and I went through everything that was left, I knew the fridge had been full, and she said to me, "Listen here, little woman, you didn't buy all that food just for me, you bought it for all of us. Once one of us has got the food, we all have the food. Those children out there are just as hungry as my children are in this house, so," she said, "don't come up here with your high-falutin' ideas of thinking you're doing me a favour, otherwise you can just piss off now." That was the most marvellous thing she ever said to me because if she could talk to me like that it showed me she really cared and that she wanted me to learn how things were done, not how to *be* but how to *show* I'm Koori.'

. . . .

'In the white culture not to look someone in the eye all the time that they're talking to you is rude; it's like you're not paying attention. But to look Aboriginal people in the eye the whole time you're talking to them is rude, because you're staring at them. That was really hard to get used to. It takes a long time to accept that something you learned as good manners in one culture is wrong in another, a long time to be able to do that and feel comfortable about doing it. It's like being in a no-man's-land in a way, because you don't know Aboriginal ways enough to feel comfortable and to know that you don't sort of stick out as someone who doesn't know quite what they're doing half the time. You're trying to watch other people and trying not to make mistakes and laugh at the wrong things . . . your whole body language is different. I'm sure I stick out like a sore thumb to people and they wonder, they think, this woman's a bit strange. Also I found that I lost a lot of contact with the white people I'd spent a lot of time with. That was a long process, partly because they didn't understand why it was so important to me to find out where I was from and also because it became an absolute obsession that I just had to know everything that was to do with who I was. And because most of the white people I knew didn't really understand that, I lost a lot of contact with them. You're a bit in limbo for a long time, I think.'

. . . .

'There's a natural bond that I feel toward Aboriginal people that when I was thinking white was never there. I've re-discovered that. You'll just nod, even if you don't know them, if you see them somewhere, in a restaurant or in a pub, or walking down the street. It's "Cous" or "Sis" or "Brother". You just do it.'

. . . .

'Aboriginal people are getting a lot stronger. They're feeling like their own people. They're uniting more. And they're doing a lot to rejuvenate the culture, just bring it to people's eyes. Once people know about where they come from—their country, their tribes—and they've met their families, then they've got it inside, and they know a little bit about traditional society and how traditional people lived: that's all they need.'

. . . .

'I want to say that I feel I'm regaining my Aboriginality. To me at the moment it means that I know where I'm from, I know who my people are, I'm starting to know who all my relations are and to meet them and get to know them as my aunts and uncles and cousins and my grandfather. I'm learning very slowly the history of the area that I'm from and it *is* a sense of belonging, and unless you've felt that you *don't* belong, it's really hard to explain how important it is and how precious it is knowing where I'm from.'

'When we got to Arambi Mission I was told to stand and look all around, which I did, and they said "Now, all of that's yours". It's all bounded by natural boundaries. None of it, before the *gubs* (white people) got here anyway, none of it was sub-divided for individual use.

'This is part of the land rights question. We never *had* sub-divided for individual ownership: that territory was bounded by natural boundaries.'

. . . .

'I had to know the history, to know where I came from and to be really knowledgeable. There are a lot of Aboriginal people that wouldn't know what I know, although they know it in a different way than I do. A lot that I know is from books, but they know it because they've lived it or their father or grandfather lived it and it's been passed down that way.

'I have to know things because when you get with Aboriginal people they talk about the old times a lot and you like to be able to participate, too. It's good to sit there and listen and learn; it's also good if you know a little bit, even if it is from a book.'

. . . .

'As an Aboriginal person it will give me something to identify myself by to know that I do have a family. When I'm with other fellow Aboriginals I feel a certain bond, a certain magic. I feel like I'm part of their family. It's a wonderful feeling, actually: a feeling of joy, a feeling of pride.'

. . . .

'Aboriginality means to me that you come from the land. It's your land, Australia, the trees, the grass, the seas, the deserts, the rainforests, are all linked with yourself. It's something nobody can take away from you.'

White Man Say We Have No History

'We didn't have any history according to the white man. We're one of the poor old races that didn't have anything in writing so it's only hearsay. If you put it in writing it's history.

'There's so many young people who ask, what were we like? Who were our mothers and fathers? What were our tribal names? What was our link in our tribes? I'd like to see our young people learn their traditional ways again so they could put a value on their own people instead of having to value the European value of life.'

. . . .

Brewarrina is a small country town in the north of New South Wales. To Europeans, that's all it is. But Aborigines have a history in the area going back five thousand years. It was one of the biggest of the tribal meeting places on the east of the continent. Intricately constructed stone fish traps provided food for thousands of tribal people. They gathered there for ceremonies and to renew contact with relatives. Present day Aborigines are planning a cultural centre overlooking the ancient fish traps to record the history of the people. It will also inform other Aborigines and Europeans about the rich cultural heritage of the area.

'The museum was my idea in the first place. It's my dream story and it was all created by me and a friend of mine and we decided we'd try and recreate Aboriginal culture in the north-west of New South Wales. Our theme was the Dreamtime stories of the people. When the land was a desert and there was no water and there was no river, Baiame, the creator, came up the river, making it. Digging the river, his spirit dogs made the Paroo, other spirit dogs went up the Warrego, he came here, and each place he went to he was helping people as he formed the river. When he came to Brewarrina he made the rocks, taught them how to catch fish by making the fish traps, and on leaving Brewarrina he left his footprint in the rock, which is still there today—an enormous thing 20 feet by 30 feet. And so that was the theme of our museum—that we create the Dreamtime stories of Baiame and other Dreamtime stories to create something that will make everyone aware of their traditions and make people proud of being Aborigines again.'

The river flows swiftly when there's been rain. That water covers the Aboriginal fish traps that have existed for an estimated five thousand years. Some of them are now destroyed. The rocks were used to make causeways and crossings in the 1880s when paddleboats went up the Darling River.

It's interesting to reflect that all that time in that five thousand years up till very recently there would have been Aboriginal families camped around the area, sure of being able to catch their dinner in the fish traps that had been built by their ancestors. Those fish traps now are not in use but they're still a very important part of the cultural heritage of the Aboriginal people of Brewarrina.

'Dreamtime is as long as we've been there and how long that is I don't know, but we'd have to say thousands of years. You'd have five hundred yards and a hundred yards across the water and that's the size of the traps. They were made out of stones running across the river, like sheepyards in a way, and you'd have the catching pens you'd hunt your fish into and then you'd get them into one yard and close it off, and you'd hunt them into another yard where the water was shallow, and then you'd gradually get them into where you could go and spear them or nullah them or knock them out some other way. Apparently they were owned by the Ngemba. The fish traps were controlled by the Ngemba tribe and they would invite you here—when I say 'invite you', I mean invite other tribes when the fish were plentiful. There are records of [what] I'm saying—that there were four or five thousand Aborigines at one time in Brewarrina when the fish were running. They'd come here for their ceremonies and get together and enjoy their traditions of meeting and playing and having fun, like they do today—swap yarns and talk and get to know relations and meet again after they'd been walking around for the year or years or whatever time.

'The yards, the traps were actually there, it didn't need any knowledge or anything to set them up. There are the outlines of the original traps. I can remember [some old men] talking about the old fishery and that's where some of the biggest corroborees were, on the river bank.

'The old people would meet there. But a tribe couldn't come across another tribe's boundaries unless they were invited to do so. All that's part of the old people. They'd meet up from the fishery and invite the other tribes to come down—tribes from the Culgoa and further beyond Bourke and Enngonia and those places. It was a very special place in the lives of the old people. I'd love to see it done up again. If the old traps were there it would always remind you of the old times, the old people.'

. . . .

'Once we knew a lot of stories. There were a lot of tribal Aborigines who knew good stories, mythical stories, if you like, that were told to us. But even our people after a while disbelieved these tribal people. No doubt a lot of the stories were mythical but they were very good and had a lot of good meaning to them. The old chap that told me one particular story was Mullacky Barnes who was our uncle, our old tribal uncle and a wonderful old Aboriginal. His wife Dolly—she was a lovely old woman—died. The legend used to go like this: There was the 'time to go home voice'. It was a mythical voice, and where this voice sung out 'time to go home' was at a place called the *mirrigunnah*. *Mirri* means dog in Ngemba and *gunnah* means waterhole. And out of this waterhole came Merioola, the spirit dog. Of course we never ever heard this voice—'time to go home'. It was a mythical voice. And as the Merioola came out of the *mirrigunnah*—this was the waterhole—the Merioola was the size of, say, a domestic cat, but as it climbed up the bank it grew in size until it was the size of a Shetland pony and it disappeared. It didn't matter where we were in the bush with these people, just before sundown this voice would sing out, 'Time to go home', this mythical voice. And when the sun got to treetop level in the west we'd get a premonition, if that's the word. Somebody would say 'Time to go home'. And if we were eight or ten miles from the Mission we'd be gone, back to the camp. And I was told by my old uncle that this was a method to keep the kids out of danger after dark, and it was a disciplinary thing, if you like, that all the kids were back at camp before sundown. And he told me that when the whites first came into this part of the country there were dozens of cases of white kids being drowned and lost in the bush country. And all the years as a young boy I never knew of one case of an Aboriginal child being lost on that part of the Mission or being drowned. That might have been a frigtening story to some of the kids, but it was a good way to keep them out of danger. So that was one mythical story that I knew, and there were others that were like that.'

. . . .

'My father originally came down from the Warrego area—that's Queensland. He came down, and his two brothers, Ben and Alfie, and his sister Ruth. Their real name was Goodgebah— their tribal name—because they were tribal people. When they came down to Cunamulla, old Arthur Shillingsworth adopted them—three brothers and a sister—and put them in his name. That how my people come to be Shillingsworth today. One of the biggest tribal places was Dungowan. There were many tribes there at the time when my father met my mother. She was a Bailey. He married her but then the police—troopers— sent the trucks out to round up all Aboriginals and put them in one place on the Mission. They took them all from Dungowan. My mother and my father took off—ran away— and they couldn't find them. They even had policemen—you know, troopers on horseback. They rounded the rest up and took them up there to Angledoole. That was the next big Mission to Dungowan. They brought in everybody from everywhere, Kamilaroi, Eurelaroi—all the Aboriginal people, even from Tibooburra. They took all the Aboriginal people and put them in one big yard in Brewarrina and made them live there. They sent everyone to the Mission—all the different tribes—and they couldn't lead their own life. They tried to make them walk about in white people's clothes—tin buttons on their shirts and braces on their trousers and things like that. They used to come along and split up the different tribes.'

. . . .

'The original Aboriginal tribal area was in Brewarrina itself, at the fisheries. There were the two tribes that met there, the Morowori and the Ngemba. The Aborigines weren't mugs even in the tribal days. They knew where the high country was, and the flooded areas, and so Brewarrina was the spot these people lived at. When the settlers came into those areas they were automatically pushed off that higher ground there. And

22

of course they were shifted out miles upstream from Brewarrina to a settlement called the Mission.'

. . . .

'There was a free issue of government rations—what we called three-eight-and-a-quarter, it was. There was eight pounds of flour, three pounds of sugar and a quarter pound of tea. We'd line up with our little roll-out bags and a few milk tins and those sort of things and get our ration. There was a free issue of tobacco—plug tobacco—for the older people, and the fine cut packets for the younger men that smoked.'

. . . .

'In those times there was plenty of rabbits there and every afternoon me and the boys, all of us young fellers, would go up what we called the "hard bank" and we'd camp out of a night. We'd go up there in the sandy banks to what they call the retreat. We'd go up there to get rabbits and that— we'd knock 'em with a stick. And there were plenty of fish then, at the time. We'd camp out there on the river bank and set our lines of a night time and sit back there all night and hunt again the next morning before coming home.'

. . . .

'The native fish which were there in large schools at the time were easily caught. We used to have a natural weed that grew from the edge of the water out on both sides, something like eight to ten feet out on both sides. So at different times of the year, especially in the winter months when the fish would stop running, there was always a source of food that we could harvest, if you like, from the weeds around about. One method that we used was to get a forked stick, a big stick, and put it down in the weeds and twist the stick around and, of course, there'd be three or four of us onto this stick, and we'd pull it out onto the bank and you'd pull the weeds out and in turn you'd pull beautiful big shrimps and blue crayfish and small native fish that only grew from about six to eight inches at full growth. When they'd come out—and there'd be a dozen of us along the river pulling these out for the older people—they'd be a source of food there all day for us. So that was another source of food that we used to get there on the old river.'

. . . .

'We used to go out a lot as kids, not so much with the men, we used to go out with the old women, and they used to have what they called a *gooli*. Some of them still had the skins they'd made into *goolis* but the government blankets, the free issue blankets that we used to get, were turned into *goolis*. They used to just chuck them over the back of their shoulders and, of course, they'd carry a lot of stuff in there. If there were small kids around some of them bounced up into the *goolis* and the women would carry them around like that. But they were great gatherers of food. The women did all those sort of things.'

. . . .

'I was taken away when I was eight years old and I didn't come back until I was about seventeen.

'I can just remember getting in the car—the Welfare man put me in the car, and was taking me away and Mum was there waving and I was crying for her. And I couldn't go back because they were taking us away. I still don't know today why they took us away. Two sisters went before me, and then I went and then my other sister, and then the smallest one went and we all ended up in the same place, Coota[mundra].'

. . . .

24

'There were quite a few kids taken in the latter years, you know, around the late 'fifties. Poor old Hilda had three children taken off her from the Mission and sent to Cootamundra and another old lady here had two boys taken. I think there was remorse and sorrow here for the children that were taken. People didn't like it, but those were the laws in those days, and the boss, the manager, had the full say in anything. If he said they had to go, well, that was it.'

. . . .

'She didn't talk about it much when we came back. She was just glad to see us, I think. She said she used to go up to the station all the time and see if we were there, but we weren't. When I came back I didn't even know where to go. I thought they were still at the Mission. This woman asked me where I was going and I said "I'm going out to the Mission to see my mother", and she asked me, and I told her, and she said "Oh, I'll take you down". And we just got off the train and [Mum] came out, running out crying, when she saw me.'

. . . .

'The police were always there to enforce [the law], even up till I was fifteen. We used to live just over here and police came round, you had no say in anything, they were the law and they could walk into your place and we were brought up to be scared of them.'

. . . .

'I believe the New South Wales Police Force was equipped with Harley Davidson motor cycles at the time in the mid-1930s, and they used to have a motorbike with a sidecar on in Brewarrina, and it used to have the Sergeant and another constable and another guy ' iving. Two used to come to the

Mission and each one would have a rifle—I think it might have been a repeater .22 or pump-action rifle. If there were any dogs there in the street they'd be automatically shot. But we were a wake-up to the police coming out. We'd put a leash on them and away we'd go into the timber with them and we'd hide there until the police went. We had to do that because it was our only way of getting meat—emus and kangaroos. It was impossible to run them down by foot so the only way that we could get them was with the kangaroo dogs, we used to call them. They were a source of getting food, if you like, for a lot of our people there on the Mission.'

. . . .

'We used to make a *boondi*. It was a stick and it was about two foot long, a very streamlined shape, a thin handle, and it was well balanced and it was a throwing stick. When the rabbits were in millions in that part of the country we became very skilled with these particular sticks and you'd start a rabbit up out of a squat, a squat being a roly-poly (a weed ball), and three or four guys would get around this rabbit and start him up and he'd come out, bounce out, and you'd anticipate his move, of course. You'd judge his distance and you'd throw two or three feet in front of him and you'd get him every time. So I'd say that our tribal people were very, very skilled with these particular sticks. You'd knock the goannas that lived there off the trees, too, with them. We used to have other small marsupial animals there. We had the ·*bilby* in that area forty years ago but they're gone now. He was a little kangaroo-type animal, long ears, something like a hare. But he was very good eating.'

. . . .

'I learned from men, some of them in their sixties and seventies, to make these particular weapons that I make now. If you

joined in the workshop—the workshop I'm talking about then
was out on the woodheap—all they had was a tomahawk and
a rasp, and if you toed the mark and sat down there with
these people and wanted to learn to make something, you were
free to do so. You could pick up a stick and work it and they'd
teach you what to do. But if there was anybody playing up
they'd whisk them right out of it. We weren't allowed even
to call them by their first names. It always had to be "Uncle".'

. . . .

'There were quite a few old fellers out there, I can remember,
but we couldn't go near them—we'd have to walk past them,
we couldn't walk in front of them or anything like that. We'd
have to walk at the back, we couldn't put our shadow on them
or anything. They were pretty strict with the young people.'

. . . .

'There were a lot of corroborees there. We used to help paint
the people up, even though we were fair-skinned Aborigines.
I don't know how we looked with the tribal people painted
up and whatever, but we used to get in there and do the dances
with them, as boys. They used to mix the ochre with the gum
and in later years they used to get hobby glue and mix it with
the ochre—that gave it its sticky substance, I suppose. We had
all sorts of colours—there were about seven or eight different
colours of ochres. One particular mineral we used to call *dohra*.
We used to get it off the bank of the river and it would be
chucked in the hot fires, pulled out and of course it was crushed
up and mixed with water and it made a very good white paint.
Even though our culture was gone then, there was a lot of
incentive from those older people that used to have the
corroborees there on different animals and whatever. And, of
course, when there were a couple of emus killed and brought
back into the Mission they'd be cooked and everybody'd get

a feed and there'd be a corroboree that night and they'd perform the day's hunting and they were quite good.'

. . . .

'I loved going out there, especially walking around the old graveyard and down the old bend there where we used to fish. But now all those things are gone, all the old people. But it brings back memories when I do go out there. Before, we roamed all over here and hunted, and they're . . . the places where the old people met. To me, it's where I was brought up and where I'd love to spend the rest of my life.'

. . . .

'We've got our culture, we've still got our old ways of living. We might live in a white man's home but we still have our black way, an Aboriginal way, because we live our life. My tribe is Morowori, my father tribe, and I take after my father, because my father's name is Muri Goodgebah and that means a flower or a tree. This is my land. We own this land, us Aboriginals. We were first here, before Captain Cook came. This is my land, here, where I look. We own all this, every little bush, every little tree, every log, every stick, every little bit of flower. You see those big flowers? Emus are getting fat now and they're ready to lay. We tell by the flowers because they're getting near springtime. This is our land. This not your land.'

Language Is Our Lifeblood

.'When I first heard CAAMA and I heard somebody, I think it was Kenny Madden, read the news, I thought to myself, that's my language. Now I want to hear more being said, being read . . . I'm really proud of it, because it's my language that's being read to make us understand and to know more what's going on.'

. . . .

CAAMA (The Central Australian Aboriginal Media Association) has been broadcasting in Aboriginal languages to the people of Central Australia since 1984. For many in remote settlements it is the only information they get from the outside world. Although there is a danger that broadcasting major languages will smother the lesser-used ones and cause them to disappear more quickly, there is no doubt that hearing your own language on radio and television contributes to a sense of identity and pride.

'We started off with three major languages and we seem to be able to cover from Tennant Creek down to the Great Australian Bight because Pitjatjantjara is fairly large, Arrente is one of the largest Aboriginal languages in Australia and Warlpiri is a very distinct language group. But we're doing the dialects of Arrente, which is the country that we're broadcasting in, we're broadcasting in Amatchera and because we're broadcasting to the country of the Kaidija people at Allekurung we also broadcast in Kaidija as well. We need to do Allywarra, which is another dialect of Arrente, and we're hoping to do Warrumunga, which we're broadcasting in Tennant Creek.

'There has been criticism about using major languages like

Arrente, Warlpiri and Pitjatjantjara at the expense of the smaller languages. The people who study language feel that the other languages will get swallowed up if we maintain these big languages all the time.'

So is there a policy to try and diversify as much as possible?

'Certainly, and what's been happening is that people doing the traditional stories—the oral history that we're collecting—speak in their own language, so they are being broadcast quite regularly. English may sometimes be the third or fourth language for some people around here—most people speak three or four dialects. We find that we can put three completely different languages on. We've got good broadcasters who can understand other languages and they can joke and laugh in two different languages.'

. . . .

'When I heard that these other languages were going on the air, I said, "Why not try my language?". I saw Phillip and asked him if I could come down here to do the Kaidija show. I didn't really know how to speak Kaidija properly. I had to go back to Barrow Creek and stay for a fortnight on Neutral Junction station, that's the station we were brought up at. I picked up all my languages again and now I can speak properly, I think. The old people back at Newtlands and at Barrow Creek like to hear me talking in Kaidija. The older people down at the camp all have wirelesses now, so they just wait for when I start talking and they turn all their wirelesses on just to hear what I've got to say for them. I think it's important for the Kaidija to go on because the other kids growing up like to speak it, I suppose, and the old people like them to carry on talking their own lingo.'

. . . .

'I do CAAMA news in Warlpiri and also in English sometimes, but mainly in Warlpiri—everything I read in the paper is interpreted in Warlpiri. When we do these things they listen to it; it's good that somebody who speaks that language can tell them what's going on round the world. First, without the CAAMA, they didn't know what was being said in English; only a few could understand it—those who've been in schools.'

. . . .

A lot of the programs are request programs and a lot of the requests are European songs, aren't they?

'Yes, it's very hard to explain to non-Aboriginal people that Aboriginal music is not broadcastable, it's not a three-minute song. An Aboriginal song can go on for six months if it's done correctly. Say the migration tracks of the birds—they're sung over right the way from the desert to the Gulf of Carpentaria and back again. And while that migration period might take six months, people are singing those birds across all the time as they're moving. Each family takes it up as the birds migrate wherever they are. If they're here in Alice the families here are doing it. If you go up a bit further to Bushy Park, other families are responsible for it and they keep singing the songs and they're defferent all the way along. It goes right up to Boroloola and the birds come back, circle back and come back to the desert to lay their eggs again. So that story can be six months long. And it's really hard to take a three-minute snitch out of songs that go on and on and on. If it was sung for Alice Springs it may go for three days. The songs are sung for three days with no sleep. People just sit there and sing as the birds go over. That is one story that is called the Atuthura story and it goes from the desert here to the Gulf of Carpentaria. The stories and the songs are both together, you have to learn the songs which are part of the story.'

If you're trying to describe your traditional stories, is it possible to tell them in English or can you only tell them in your own language?

'When there is something very difficult, a very hard word, sometimes we have to find a very similar word that can fit in that traditional word or corroboree or whatever that thing is. It's very hard and it's one of the things that Yabba people always worried about—putting similar things really close to something that's really hard for them to try to explain or to show.

'If there is something that I have to show—for example, the designs for a traditional painting—I would use language, a bit of the language; but if it's for white people it would be very hard for me to try and explain or try to make them see the picture or understand the picture. It's very hard for a European bloke to get what the picture is saying or what the picture is telling; it's very hard. English sometimes doesn't have the right word, and English sometimes doesn't fit into some of our traditional designs.'

. . . .

'Children who don't know the language, who don't know how to speak, how to tell stories, should try to get someone to teach them how these things are said and what these stories mean.'

. . . . .

How important is language in preserving the culture?

'Oh, it's our lifeblood. This is what we tell the young people: You have to know your language because you'll never be able to learn your Dreaming and if you don't know your Dreaming you can't identify where you belong. If you don't identify where you belong you may as well say you're dead. As an Aboriginal person you have to know your language to be able to learn your Dreamings.'

Is English a very inadequate sort of tool to describe Aboriginal Dreamings and lifestyles and things like that?

'I think so, because I think that the word dreaming in English is sleeping—you know, sleeping what you dream about. But for us it's got nothing to do with that whatsoever. Dreaming is the tracks that you are responsible for. You grow up, then you have to maintain it spiritually. You've got to maintain it through not over-using it; you've got to do the ceremonies for the different animals; you've got to do ceremonies for human beings; and as you grow and as you get older you learn your responsibilities to that area. As you get older still, and as you marry into different families, you take on the responsibility of other people, and as your children have children you take on the responsibilities of other Dreamings—their Dreamings, the children's Dreamings, which might go a different way from yours. It just depends who you marry. And it's all really very interesting and fascinating.'

But the term dreaming in English almost means lying back and doing nothing, whereas you're talking about a very active process.

'Yes, very busy, and you never stop learning. The Aboriginal currency in the traditional way was knowledge. The more Dreamings a person knew or the more tracks he had become responsible for, the more powerful that person became or the more knowledgeable that person became. And you never stopped learning. If you were the person looking after that track or that Dreaming, you were the one that was looked after. People fed you and you became responsible for the stories for that land and knowing all the things about that land and knowing the secret, sacred ceremonies for that land. The more you knew, the more you got looked after wherever you went because when the right time came for you to teach, you were then looked after by the people who you were responsible for.'

. . . .

'A long time ago people would all meet up and there were some areas that had their corroborees . . . to do with our cultural stories and this type of thing. So we've got to look at the political aspects of things because, of course, those gatherings were for political purposes, between tribes or between family groups. Now we look at how we send a message out to the community. I know if it's my language being spoken I will listen to that quite closely. But English . . . you can hear English and you don't really take notice of it. But when you hear your own language and what's being spoken in your own language, you do take a lot more notice. Since we've had CAAMA, the people are more aware of what politics is about because we can interpret exactly what the people are saying and we can let the community know what people are saying.'

. . . .

'Most of the Aboriginal Community here are semi-literate or illiterate. We've had communications skills since the beginning of time here and our communications skills are by word of mouth and also the visual thing . . . like most of the news here in the Northern Territory, because the Aboriginal community is a large part of the population most of the news is on the Aboriginal issues. We can get these news items and press statements and all this type of thing out to the communities in their languages with proper, skilled interpreters that can relay the message to the community.

'If a member of the ruling government says something on Aboriginal issues, that gets interpreted and goes out. If people, say, from the ALP put out a message, that also goes out and the importance is that the community in the outlying areas know what's going on in the major towns such as Alice Springs, Katherine, Tennant Creek and Darwin. They've got information directly out to them in a language they can understand. So the language broadcasting here at CAAMA is one of the most important parts of our role in self-determination—the survival of the language, whether it be Pitjatjantjara or Warlpiri or Amadgera or Kaidija or Luritja. Because we use those languages up here in the Central Australian region every day, it helps self-esteem within the community: we have our own language, we can identify with our own relations, extended family groups and things like that. That plays a major, important part in the community. We can converse in about three or four different Aboriginal languages before we can converse in English. There might be an Arrente bloke sitting down and listening to Walpiri news and he'll understand it, or a Kaidija woman sitting listening to Luritja news. You know, it's direct communication to the old men and old women of the country and we tell them what's going on there.'

. . . .

'I'm a member of the Aboriginal community here in Alice Springs and I have been here most of my life and we've had a "beat the grog" campaign going on. Well, being a member of the community who has a high profile in the community, I go around and I look at things such as shops and grog outlet places. But now people are buying more tucker than they used to do before, more blankets, more clothes. Just through the communication of an anti-grog publicity campaign—'Why drink so much?'—the people are not drinking so much and that in itself has proved to me personally that it's happening.

In our land rights issues we come on this wireless here and we talk: we talk about what they are going to be doing in Canberra, about our land rights act. We went from Alice Springs with 400 people representing the tribe—that was through information going from this little wireless out to the communities in the languages explaining what was going on. The people being involved knew what the amendments and changes were. The community knows about what's going on now, the community knows next time that their vote is going to be worth a lot more than it was previously because we're aware of the issues.'

. . . .

'From the outside it appears that we're just a request station— you know, people writing in—but that's part of being Aboriginal, letting everybody know where you are and who you are and whose family you belong to and all that sort of thing. But as people see the strength of the station and what it can do, by having the language and by our young people being able to listen to their own language, it's a lesson in itself. It says, my language is important. Whereas, before, kids were saying, 'It's not important; we won't be able to get anywhere with our own language; what's the use of learning language', now we've got the opportunity to hear our own language; it's not being pushed aside.'

What sort of response do you get from those people on outlying stations who hear their own language over the airwaves?

'When we first broadcast, I've seen women cry when they heard their language on the radio, they were just so excited, laughing and joking. I don't think people could manage now without having CAAMA or without having a radio station that broadcast their own language.'

Learning Two Ways

'It's important that the children learn their own language because it *is* their own language. Why teach English to Aboriginal kids if they've got their own language?

· ·

Yipirinya school was the first independent Aboriginal school in Australia. It is in Alice Springs and its intention is to teach Aboriginal culture to Aboriginal children, thereby encouraging children to keep their culture strong.

The Literature Development unit at the school makes books for the children to learn from. Dreamtime stories and contemporary oral history related by the elders living in and around Alice Springs provide the raw material.

'The first thing the Aboriginal Council does is make decisions about bush trips. There are a couple of elders who go out on bush trips, and camping out sometimes. They tell stories about the land and everything that came in the Dreamtimes that the children should still learn. We take pictures, photos, and make videos, then bring them back to the school and work out how to make the books. We make a recording, too, and keep it in a file in the Literacy Centres, so that when we start working on books we can just take out the things we want to write about to teach the children in school. The stories that we write from the tapes will become lessons later to make books.'

· · · ·

'We check the story out with the person who told it to the children to make sure that everything is all right to be written down, and then we start writing it. We also check with the linguists working here, just to make sure. In the old days people never wrote any Dreamtime stories or the stories that the old people tell us. We just heard what they told us.'

. . . .

'It's important that the children learn their own language because it *is* their own language. Why teach English to Aboriginal kids if they've got their own language? They should learn and be taught in their own language so they can learn more quickly and it's their first language. It makes it strong with themselves. They'll be fluent then to speak and to write it. They can have anything if they know the language, make a book of their own or film, make a video . . . especially in teaching their own kids, generation after generation.'

. . . .

The Aboriginal Council were emphatic that control of Yipirinya should rest with them and not with the Government Education Department. The five-year fight for registration which gave access to funding included an appeal to the Supreme Court. In September 1983 Yipirinya officially became the first independent Aboriginal School.

'You know, we had big trouble before. Sometimes we would send the kids down the path and say, "You have to go to school, not play around the street or down the creek there. Some of the white kids [used to say], "Hey, this is not an Aborigine school. It's for whites". The kids were ashamed then and didn't want to go to school. At the government school they didn't help Aboriginal people.

'When I sent the kids in the morning to school and they got money for lunch, the white kids always took the money away from them. They went straight home, they weren't happy at that school. The white kids were cheeky all the time, took their money and hit them. That's why the kids always ran away. They didn't learn anything, Aboriginal or anything.

White people's way is all they learnt at that school.

'At Yiririnya school they're learning two ways. They speak fluent Arrente and that's why we have an Aboriginal teacher to teach them so they can understand. The kids come every day and I'm happy and the kids are very happy.'

. . . .

Eli Rabunja is an Arrente elder and the Foundation President of the School Council:

'The Education Minister asked me "Hey, Eli, why did you start this Aboriginal school? You should go through the government school". [I said,] "I think this way: I've got to ask the Aboriginal people what they're going to do with their kids, give them a government education or put them in the school. I've got to ask them first." "Well, that's all right", the Minister said, "Where are you going to get the money?" I said, "We're going to ask the government for the money." There was trouble all the time before we were registered at Yipirinya. Every fortnight government people came from Darwin, Canberra, all the Education people. After five years we were registered. Now we can't leave this school. We started it, and we'll just keep going with our kids, teaching.'

. . . .

'When I first came to work at Yipirinya the school wasn't registered yet and at the time we were fighting for registration. It's gone a long way from when I first came to work here. It's improving every year, I think. There's about three languages being taught in the school now.'

. . . .

'It's important for the kids to go to the bush and learn everything like taking witchitty grubs, collecting all the bush food and the bush honeys.'

39

'I was living in the bush a long time with my grandmother and I'm teaching my kids the same as my grandmother told me, all the stories, the bush things and camping out and finding bush food and meat.'

. . . .

The children are taught about the various medicinal qualities of the gum tree. They break off the branches and the outside bark to have a look at the sap and see the colour of things. They're being taught what these things can be used for. It's all part of being educated as an Aboriginal at Yipirinya school.

Just north of Alice Springs in a little bit of roadside bush the kids bang pieces of bark with a couple of stones to crumble it up and then put it in billy cans. Another group of kids make a fire. The idea is to boil the bark in some water and then use the liquid for sores—sore eyes and sores on feet and legs.

The mixture boils for ten or fifteen minutes, then is left in the wind to cool for a while. The kids dip cloth or tissues into the mixture and wash their legs with it. Activities like applying the liniment to people's sores and cooking witchetty grubs are filmed for use in a classroom later on.

'I'm writing those stories about bush medicine and trees and plants for Yipirinya on my tape in my language. After, I'll write it in English and make a book for kids to read, Yipirinya kids.'

. . . .

Eli Rabunja: 'Education means everything . . . that's why you've got to learn. We just take the kids to the bush first and show them food and water, where you go to find them, and take them around. That's education for Aboriginal people. In our own culture there is a lot to teach the children about their own ways—there's both Western and the Aboriginal ways. But by education in European ways, we mean schooling and stuff like that—jobs, how to survive.

'Today they think two ways. It's got to be like that. We have two people here—white and black. Aboriginal people can learn something from white cultures and white people can learn from Aboriginal cultures. They've got to be learned together.'

. . . .

'My tribe is Arrente. My grandfathers are all Arrente and my kids are all Arrente.

'Alice Springs is really Mparntwe which means the Dreaming of the caterpillar. There's three different kinds of caterpillar but the Yipirinya is the main caterpillar here in Alice Springs. The story of caterpillars seems to be one of the histories of Alice Springs. Another caterpillar came from Western Australia and the third came from the North and they joined into Yipirinya. They started to scout around looking for food, then they travelled on to Emily Gap. Hills and trees here represent Yipirinya, like, for instance, these coolibah trees where they've built the water resource. That's caterpillar Dreaming. They would travel and all these hills represent the Yipirinya and the caterpillar. That's their track and they travelled East to Emily Gap where they found a home. It's a place where nobody can go, not even the initiated men. It's a special place, it's Amekameke.

'At Emily Gap you can see paintings that represent all three caterpillars. I usually take the kids around all Yipirinya and I tell them the story of the caterpillar so they can keep it always and it can't be lost. It's still important. It can't be wasted away, it's got to be there always and passed on from generation to generation.

'We still look after Emily Gap and we get a good bit of help and support from the National Parks and Wildlife and Conservation Commission. They help us support and look after it. If that was destroyed, many of our elders would be dead and gone. There'd be a lot of sicknesses and you'd see many of our people dying away. It's where our strengths are kept. Once our important places are left untouched we'll all be okay. The children understand this. I usually pass it on to them and we keep it as a record at Yipirinya school. So when I'm dead and gone the story and the history of the Yipirinya will be there always.'

. . . .

'There's oral history being told by our old people, the elders, about the first white man, and I've actually got that from my father and it's been written in the book. We try and encourage the old people to tell us what happened in the past and they've got lots of stories to tell. They didn't really know what it was when they first saw a white person. They thought he was covered in some sort of paint or web, cobwebs. They said, "It's got two legs and looks like us, but the colour's wrong". Some were frightened but they hid behind the trees and had a look. They just saw this white man going past and they were actually living up the north road—a place called Berts Plain—where my father used to live, and my grandfathers. That's the first time they saw a white man.

'It was the explorer, Stuart. He came past through Orange Creek and went on to Jay Creek and then came into Alice Springs area, and on to Old Telegraph Station. He met other old people there and he travelled up north and that's when he saw my family sitting down and they said, "Oh, whatever is this? A spirit or whatever?". And he just went past and talked a little and they couldn't understand what he was saying.

'Some people who lived in Central Australia used to go down south, visiting relations, and from time to time my family used to hear there were white people down south but they didn't actually see them, so for some of them it might have been a frightening sight, the first time seeing a white person.

'You only read in white history books about white explorers

and first transports and so on. You never hear about Aboriginal people. That is why we try to get all these stories down in a book so the children can read about what happened before to our people.'

The Spirit of Musgrave Park

'This is my perception of Musgrave Park—as an unspoilt segment of a once great spiritual piece of land that has been spiritual to a large number of tribes from this specific area of Australia . . . it is also a haven for me, where I can be an Aborigine without stress, without being ridiculed by Europeans, and being looked down on as sub-human by Europeans.'

. . . .

Musgrave Park is a square piece of grassy land the size of two, perhaps three, city blocks among factories and run-down cottages in South Brisbane. There's the usual toilet block in one corner. The streets bordering it are fairly heavily trafficked and there are even parking meters down one side. But there are some trees, big shady trees that are nice to sit under, even on a rainy day when they give shelter from the rain. There's a rough kind of football ground in the middle and a cricket pitch in one corner. Altogether it's a fairly typical inner city park.

During the Commonwealth Games in 1982 thousands of Aboriginal people from all States gathered in Musgrave Park to attract international attention to Aboriginal rights. The protests were peaceful and successful, and the park became the focus for the black struggle in Queensland.

'It was really a magical feeling having Aboriginal people coming from all around Australia. We had people from Tasmania, the Northern Territory and Western Australia—and all other parts of Australia, even from our community reserves. A tent city was established. It was quite a big tent city: it had marquees and things like that for people to live in, and people also slept in cars, and were put up in hostels and church buildings. We

44

took people into our own private homes as well because there were a lot of elderly people and we didn't want them being subject to police harassment at that time, or the white harassment that was around. There's only one particular area of the park that was used all the time, which is the closest part to the Brisbane River. The other area was used mainly for sport or some kind of cultural event, and we all met and stayed within the one area. Everybody lived there, sharing, contributing to how the struggle would be fought at that time, how we were going to get our messages across. It was a great landmark for Brisbane, and a great landmark for Australia, and you had thousands of Aboriginal people really working together and putting ideas together. It was just brilliant, I think, to see everybody there together.'

. . . .

From the Commonwealth Games experience came a desire to protect Musgrave Park from development and make sure it remained an open space where Aboriginal people could meet for celebrations, funerals, or to make decisions that affected the whole community. To ensure the area for future generations, the Aborigines had to document the ritual and social significance of the park. It was planned that the information would then be made into an educational kit to illustrate the importance of the park to Aboriginals, and also to add weight to requests for Aboriginal control of the area in the future. The Foundation of Aboriginal and Islander Research and Action received a research grant for the project from the Australian Government. They went to written sources, and to the Archives. But first they tapped oral memories—like these—of the Aboriginals living in Brisbane.

'I was taken to Musgrave Park by Uncle William McKenzie. I think he was ninety-four or ninety-six years of age at that time. He came and he said, "Look, this is Musgrave Park, this is a tribal ground", and he sat down and told me and Pastor Don Brady and a lot of elders in that time the history behind that certain bit in Musgrave Park. The initiations of the people [took place] there. Women came there to conceive, the battles between the different tribes were settled there, the talks were there, sitting down for peace or fighting. All the disputes were settled there. But there are a lot of things that I can't tell you, which are very sacred to me. If I did I'd be persecuted by my own people—not by the people living here but the people who are dead and gone now. It is an unwritten law that you can only say so much. But that was my first introduction to Musgrave Park by Uncle Willy McKenzie. Although I knew Musgrave Park had existed for many years, I did not know the true meaning of it.'

. . . .

'Musgrave Park has been a gathering place for my people, Aboriginal people, since the beginning of time. I know that all different tribes right throughout south Queensland have been coming to this area long before any white man or European. They've come from as far as Gympie, as far south as Southport, and as far west as Toowoomba—a lot of different tribes in the one area living peacefully at the same time. The Woolloongabba area was actually the place where they'd meet on the battlefield and sort out their differences. When someone was seriously hurt then that was more or less the end of the fight and there wasn't a total annihilation of each tribe. We lived pretty peacefully together really.'

. . . .

'These people would all gather here every four years for festivals. My tribe would participate by allocating certain areas of the Bunya Mountain for specific tribal foraging. But if someone transgressed on someone's area, the issue was settled by feats of strength or show of arms or whatever, in a controlled environment. And we'd have our corroborees, our initiations.

Where Brisbane now stands was the overall area where the allocations of the land by my people were held, and the actual ceremonies of the land allocation were made on Mount Clutha.'

. . . .

'Oral history is the most significant history from the Aboriginal people because the park has been developed in some way, and a lot of evidence has been removed from the area. But the oral history that Aboriginal people still maintain is that a bora ring existed, that there are three graves of Aboriginal people within the area, and that the path to Vulture Street runs back into the Woolloongabba where you'll find another bora ring. The history of the area, the vegetation that grew there, what Aboriginal people ate, what they used—animals and plants and those type of things—have been revealed as well.'

. . . .

'There is an abundance of evidence showing that Aboriginal people have a significant claim to make—historical and social— within the area. Written information is available in John Steel's books on Aboriginal pathways that surround the south-east Queensland area, and other written records, and it stands beside the information that the Aboriginal people have been talking about.'

. . . .

'We're doing all this research, and it's making people aware. Not all Aboriginals are aware that there are six burial grounds in Brisbane that we know of, and there are probably 100 sacred sites or bora rings. Certainly white people don't know anything about it. We're going to use this information to make people aware, but also although Aboriginal people can't claim land in Queensland, if it came to a claim, we've got evidence which could stand up in a courtroom. Musgrave is the heart of land rights, and Aboriginals are the original owners of this country, but we're not recognised as such.'

. . . .

'We'll fight in any way to retain that park. But let me make this one important point: we're only on this earth for a short time, and from there we'll go to Hell or Heaven. That's what the white men say in the Bible. But I know if I destroy this land, if I destroy these sacred sites, I've got to suffer the consequences afterwards. We'll fight politically, we'll fight violently. If necessary we'll use force to retain that park. I know blacks, and I know young blacks are prepared to do that. A lot of other blacks would probably go along with them. But, after that point of time, if we are defeated, we won't be defeated for ever.'

. . . .

'Already people have announced to me that they are prepared to get in front of the bulldozers if any of the trees were touched. They will not stand aside and let it happen. It is quite obvious from what's been told to me that the people are intending to fight. Anything that we have gained within Brisbane, throughout Australia, has only come through the blacks' struggle. So they have got nothing to lose, and a lot to gain.'

. . . .

'Musgrave Park is the heart of the community. We like to sit amongst the trees with our people. We couldn't go to a hall, we don't feel relaxed and we can't come out and say what we really want to say. [But if] we sit in Musgrave Park they will speak out, and they'll speak out in all honesty. To me Musgrave Park is the heart of Brisbane.'

. . . .

'Musgrave Park is identified by my people as a place where they could feel secure in their role as Aborigines—even though it's negative at this stage. But they are secure with each other because of their identification with an Aboriginal area, and I suppose this is a major attraction, this sense of belonging because of the Aboriginality that is identified with Musgrave Park.'

. . . .

'I've been in Brisbane for the last twenty-six or twenty-seven years and before any of these black organisations were formed, we used it as a gathering place for black people. Now if you go to Musgrave Park today you'll see black people sitting there. It's an information centre for blacks from all over Australia— or anywhere, in Queensland—who come to Brisbane looking for their friends; they go to Musgrave Park because that's the information centre. But there's something in Musgrave Park. I can understand it. *You* can't, and you can't help it because you're white. But there's something very spiritual within us in Musgrave Park. There's not a month goes by when I don't jump in my motor car and it's two miles to Musgrave Park, and sit there at two o'clock in the morning, and sit in a bora ring and speak and get the feeling from my ancestors and people who still live within me today. And to get strength and to get that closeness, I do go to Musgrave Park for that and that alone. And how I keep carrying on is because I get that strength from within myself from those people.'

. . . .

'Musgrave Park serves as a haven or a refuge for nearly all black people. So where we can't reach into white society and draw strength from white society when we're down, we can reach back into black society and draw strength from there. And the only place we can go where we can touch our mother the earth, and feel the grass and the earth and see the trees and the birds and the sky, is Musgrave Park. It's the only place where we can gather socially and be accepted. You go into a white hotel or white restaurant, or something like this, and many's the time you get rejected, or refused entry, for all sorts of reasons. They're very particular in the way they refuse you, and say, "Oh, you're wearing brown shoes, we're only allowing people who wear black shoes today—it's not because you're black, don't get me wrong. You're not wearing a tie, we're only allowing people in who are wearing a tie". Things like this.'

. . . .

'A lot of our old drones, that means old alcoholics, old "goomies", old metho kings and queens who've passed on—like my sister who was classed as the Queen of the Drones of Queensland—died in Musgrave Park. We had a service for her in Musgrave Park. Only three weeks [later] we had another service for an old bloke from Cherbourg at Musgrave Park, and that is very good. We just don't say, "Have a service at Musgrave Park". This old gentleman died about 200 miles away from here but he used to be in Musgrave Park, and [the idea] came from his own sons and daughters. "We would like a service to be held for our father in Musgrave Park." So it is something spiritual drawing them back to Musgrave Park to have the service there. There are a lot of services held there, a lot of demonstrations; there have been a lot of communications there. You know, when the blacks want to get together, today, tomorrow or next week, they call a meeting in Brisbane and right throughout south-east Queensland here, and say, "There's got to be a meeting in Musgrave Park". Blacks come from all around, and demonstrate and sit there to hear what the plan is. It's a place for people to gather, and Pastor Don Brady—to me he was the black Martin Luther King of Australia—he started his ministry there. He started to preach from Musgrave Park, and we used to have the police and white people driving past and they said, "What's this blackfeller doing speaking about the gospel of the Lord Jesus Christ—and he's speaking about land rights, and he's speaking about tribal areas. What's this man doing, this crazy man?" But let me tell you, the black people have sweet bugger all here in Brisbane, and all the service we get here in Queensland started from Musgrave Park! Musgrave Park is the gathering place for people.'

. . . .

'When a black child is three or four years old, he's cute, he's a good mate for little white kids to play with, he can't do anything wrong. But as soon as he starts to get bigger and stand out a bit, the white parents generally say to the child, "Don't bring that little black kid home any more". The little white kid—it's his best mate—he gets all upset and says, "Why not?". But there's no explanation from mum and dad. There is an explanation that's detrimental to the black person—the blacks are dirty, they've got nits in their hair, they all sleep together, and all sorts of things—and it's very down-putting to the Aboriginal people, and there's no respect for our culture, our way of life. As the black kid grows up he can't hit out at anyone else, only himself for being black. And he sees this continual rejection, continual animosity [that] is directly attributable to his blackness. And so he hates being black. The only release he has for this is through alcohol, or drugs, and so the next step is alcohol and drugs. Then he overcomes this, but the feeling of not belonging, of being unacceptable, still stays with him, still lingers there. There's no incentive for him to improve his way of life, the only place he can turn to that is familiar to him where he feels at home, where he can forget all this, is Musgrave Park. And sure, a lot of our people drink there. But if you wander around the groups that are sitting there in the park, you'll find that a lot of them aren't drinking but just sitting there talking, discussing the events that are occurring in relation to our people. It's just a social gathering on a lot of occasions. But the white man doesn't see this. He sees a group of blacks sitting there, so naturally assumes they are drinking, and plotting all sorts of mischief. The white police believe this also, and you see them continually going there with the paddy waggons and just grabbing blacks left, right and centre whether they're drunk or not, putting them in gaol and charging them with drunkenness—and so it goes on.'

· · · ·

'When I came to Brisbane, the first place I hit was Musgrave Park because I didn't know anyone around the place. I met a couple of people on the road, and the first thing they said was, "You'll see all the Murris down at Musgrave Park". So I just went down there and met all my people from where I come from.'

· · · ·

'I've been living in the park for a year-and-a-half to two years. Fifty or sixty people were living there. We had tents and everything. A couple of times the police cut the ropes so the tent fell down. Most of the time they come to hassle us. Sometimes when we are asleep they put their sirens on to wake us up, and high beam their lights in our faces. You get some white people coming around to stir us up for sleeping in the park at twelve o'clock or one o'clock in the morning. They throw stones at us and bottles while we're asleep. It isn't much good, but it's the only place where we can live.'

· · · ·

'My father used to live in Brisbane years ago, before he had any of his eleven children, and when he moved back in the

52

early 1960s, South Brisbane was still thickly populated with Aboriginal and Islander people, particularly Aboriginal people, and my father would run into destitute lost souls, lost between two cultures, losing their own identity. And they'd be drunk, hopelessly lost, didn't know what to do with their lives, living on the fringe so to speak. And he would know these people, and he'd bring them home and he'd feed them, and bath them and change their clothing. Before we knew it he was running more or less a hostel for people living in the South Brisbane area.'

. . . .

'Unfortunately, white people can never understand the beauty, the closeness, of being black. When you are black, you are never alone. You see, a stranger can come into town, broke, with just the clothes he stands up in. He'll head for Musgrave Park and tell his story to some of the people there. Well, somebody will befriend him, take him home, give him a shower, change of clothes, a bed, and he's right till he gets on his feet.'

. . . .

'I think it's the spirit of the family of Brisbane of the Aboriginal community. If I was to go back there now, the only place that I would go back to first to establish my place in that society is Musgrave Park. There I would be able to find my position within the community. It would be established there. If I wanted to meet anybody, that's where I'd have to go. If I was going to get any directions about what road I should travel or what I was going to do in relation to the struggle, or community development or to find out what the community wanted, it would be there. It's a grapevine that continually works for you. It's a place where you meet your family and stay. Your spirit is lifted again, your respect has come back.'

'People truly don't understand the significance of the South Brisbane area. Suburban Aborignals are still very much a cultural people and spiritual people, and we've got our ties to that day and age and it's been passed down through the generations. And the only bit of land, unoccupied land, at the moment is Musgrave Park and we feel very strongly about this area. It's very spiritual as well, and we've still got that tie, and we'd like to keep Musgrave Park as part of our ancestry, so to speak.'

· · · ·

'Europeans and their perception of land is based on the materialistic. They look upon land as 'my land, I own that land'. It is a commodity. Whereas Aborigines look at something as a part of the whole, a part of themselves, and they are part of that—the land. The land and they are one. This is my perception of Musgrave Park—as an unspoilt segment of a once great spiritual piece of land that has been spiritual to a large number of tribes from this specific area of Australia. This is how I perceive Musgrave Park, and it is also a haven for me, where I can be an Aborigine without stress, without being ridiculed by Europeans, and being looked down on as sub-human by Europeans. It's a sense of being me, within my own environment. This is what Musgrave Park means to me.'

· · · ·

Permission is expected soon for Aborigines to build a cultural centre on Musgrave Park which they will control. They hope that some time in the future the whole park will be controlled by an Aboriginal Council. They say, 'This park to us is like Ayers Rock to the Central Australian Aborigines'.

A Hidden History
by Bill Bunbury

In 1983 I produced a radio documentary called 'We Have to Lift Our Game' for ABC Radio's 'Background Briefing' on the circumstances surrounding the violent death of John Pat, a young Aboriginal from Roebourne in the Pilbara.

That experience provided my first close contact with Aboriginal people and made me rethink our own history and its sometimes tragic intersection with theirs. That history is also a largely hidden history, sometimes hidden even from Aboriginal people themselves, and certainly hidden from the European consciousness, even today.

That Aboriginal perspective was to emerge in an Aboriginal social history of the Australian twentieth century which I made for radio and called 'Anybody Could Afford Us', the story of the effect of placing Aboriginal children in institutions like those at Cootamundra in New South Wales and Moore River in Western Australia. That documentary looked at the impact of curfews, the denial of citizenship and the lack of employment and housing for Aboriginal people, issues which have profoundly affected them and their children.

For the narration in 'Anybody Could Afford Us' I am indebted to anthropologist Marcia Langton and political leader Rob Riley, also to Bella Yappo, Hazel Anderson, Bob Bropho, Ivan Yarran and Armold Frank, among others, whose stories illustrated that narration.

In 'Out of Sight, Out of Mind', I explored in much more detail the thinking behind the Government Settlement at Moore River, using first-hand experience. But this time I wanted to include non-Aboriginal experience as well and here I was fortunate in finding Stanley Middleton, former Commissioner for Native Welfare in Western Australia, former Assistant Commissioner Bruce McClarty, and the well-loved (by Aboriginal people) Sister Eileen, an Anglican deaconess whose frank comments to the authorities ensured her removal from Moore River.

One of the outstanding storytellers in that program was Alice Nannup, now in her late seventies, whose life epitomises the Aboriginal struggle to cope with a dominant white culture. Her story took us beyond institutions like Moore River and Cootamundra, out into the world of work on terms dictated by another society.

The next generation was represented by Shorty O'Neill and Margaret Colbung, whose stories also showed the triumph of the human spirit in difficult circumstances. In Margaret Colbung's account of schooling in the 1950s she reminded us that there are still people in our community who have not been able to overcome adversity as she did, something that could also be said of Shorty O'Neill, whose remarkable career led him to an unusual radio job, almost impossible to someone without his experience.

Finally, I will always value the time I spent with respected elder, Paddy Roe, of Broome. I was able to spend a day exploring his country, the Roebuck Plain, with Paddy and that was a rare opportunity to learn from a remarkable and generous man. His concern for the spiritual life of those who will follow him is an inspiration in itself.

For the sake of Paddy Roe and all who told their stories so willingly and with such clarity and commitment, I hope that these accounts will help to give the Aboriginal experience of our times its true place in our history.

Bill Bunbury
ABC Social History Unit, Perth 1990

Out of Sight, Out of Mind

'The food there was wicked, really. You'd get bread and scrape for breakfast, a bit of watery old soup for dinner, no such thing as meat, no such thing as sugar in your tea, no such thing as milk in your tea, and you'd get bread and scrape.'

There is a happy land, far, far away,
Where we get bread and scrape three times a day.
Bread and butter we never see
No sugar in our tea
While we are gradually
Starving away.

. . . .

That 'happy land' was the Moore River Aboriginal Settlement. Today it is an Aboriginal farm community set along the tree-lined banks of the Moore River. Almost all that remains now of the original settlement are a few ruined buildings and a chapel.

The Mission at Mogumber started in 1917 with the aim of training young people as domestic servants or farm workers. But in the 1920s Moore River became a dumping ground for unwanted Aboriginals of all ages and from all over the State. Anyone who was 'surplus to seasonal labour requirements' could be sent there. It was a way of removing unwanted fringe dwellers from country towns. Very old people and very young people went to Moore River.

The settlement overlooked a river valley. There was an open compound for adults and disciplined dormitory-style housing for children. Moore River was run by a white superintendent and patrolled by black trackers. They made sure nobody got too far if they thought of running away.

The place is so isolated—Mogumber is the nearest railway stop on the line north from Perth, 150 kilometres away—you'd hardly know it existed. Most people still don't. But many Aboriginal people have never forgotten it. Being sent to Moore River meant going to a government settlement, to be out of sight and out of mind.

'It looked like they didn't want them to mingle with the white people. They got them in one little heap. When a family came here they got as far as the compound and to me that was like a drafting yard. The lambs were kept here and the Mums and Dads were sent down to the camp.'

· · · ·

'They'd take them in truckloads. Why, I've no idea. Why they ever did it I couldn't say from that day to this.'

· · · ·

'One day I said to Mum, "Mum, why don't we go back home? I don't like this place". She said, "I wish we could because I don't like it, too. But we've got to stay here now".'

· · · ·

Sister Eileen, a Deaconess of the Church of England, went to work at Moore River in 1935 and later wrote a report highly critical of the way it was run.

'It was always a depressing place . . . The buildings were drab and gloomy, the whole atmosphere of the place was thoroughly depressing. When I arrived at the Mogumber siding I thought at first that was where the Mission would be, but instead of that it was about eight miles through sandy plain country with not a thing in sight. I felt it was terribly isolated.'

Moore River was meant to be isolated. It was the most obvious expression of government policy towards Aboriginal people. The playwright, Jack Davis, whose play No Sugar *deals with this period, says Moore River was originally meant to be a training centre:*

'For a few years, in fact it opened in 1917, it worked very well. Then we had the Depression of the 'thirties in which it really deteriorated because finance was cut back. I think you could keep an Aboriginal person in Moore River for 2/6d per week, where they used to pay 6/- a week to keep a prisoner in Fremantle Prison, so not much money was spent in Moore River at the time. And, of course, then Moore River deteriorated to such an extent that it was a home for murderers, thieves and God knows what. People who had been speared came in there and old people came there to die. It became a clearing house for Aboriginal people—a clearing house in the sense that they were sent there just to stay there and decay in mind, body and soul. That's probably what Moore River was about.'

. . . .

Moore River was only one of several government settlements in Western Australia at this time. All of them came under the control of A O Neville, Chief Protector of Aborigines, a man many of them still remember. Margaret Morgan, whose father ran a Mission at Mount Margaret in the Eastern goldfields sums up Neville's policy:

'His whole idea was to get people separated from the tribal conditions so that they would merge and absorb in the white population and we could forget that we ever had an Aboriginal problem. But I think that a lot of white people went along with it because it was doing something about the problem.'

. . . .

'I think they wanted to do away with the Aboriginal people. We had a Native Protector named Mr Neville. He was a very hard man and he was very prejudiced on the Aboriginal people. You know, he'd go up to Mount Margaret and all that area, catching half-castes and sending them to be integrated with the whites and then he wanted the black Aboriginals to die out. He said, "In time to come they're going to die out, sooner or later". He was a very hard man.'

. . . .

'It seems to me from the prevailing attitude of those days that they didn't see Aboriginal people as human beings. They saw them as, well, the lowest of the social scale and almost feelingless. It was that kind of an attitude. So I think you can't altogether say Mr Neville was that on his own. I think he mirrored the times.'

. . . .

A O Neville controlled Aboriginal affairs from 1915 to 1940, operating under State laws which regulated Aboriginal education, employment and even marriage and freedom of movement. One of Neville's successors, Stanley Middleton, closed down Moore River in 1951, handing it over to the Methodist Overseas Mission. Middleton recalls his first visit here in 1948:

'I could smell it half a mile away before I got there—the very strong, almost overpowering smell of creosote mixed with human odours and so on. I was almost shocked by the attitude of the adult inmates. These people just sat there absolutely silent and just stared. It affected me rather profoundly, because it was so obvious that they were a people who were psychologically very disturbed. In many cases they'd been kept there for so long they couldn't remember on what grounds they were originally sent there. As far as the government was concerned it was a convenient dumping ground for unwanted natives. Take Northam as an example, one of the nearest large towns. If the Chairman of the Road Board, as it was then, felt there were too many natives there, more than were required for their purposes, like the off-season between harvesting and seeding and that sort of thing, they would get the police—they didn't have to get the Department's approval—and the police would simply round them up and take them into Moore River, out of sight, out of mind.

'Now this spread right through to the North, where it was a deliberate policy on the part of the government,' through the Native Affairs Department and through the Police Department, to take away children who obviously had some sort of European ancestry amongst them, and they were taken away without any form of recourse to courts of law or anything else. Raids used to be made on pastoral property in the Pilbara and half-caste children were just scooped up and taken away and their parents would never see them again.'

. . . .

'They used to bring a lot of people away from where they lived. There were girls there from Derby, they used to bring down even the old women for some unknown reason, I don't know why. No one's ever said.'

. . . .

'The Aboriginal Affairs used to come around North, scouting for little kids to take them away from their parents. When they knew they were around, my mother and the little girls used to make sandwiches up and give them to us and we'd have to stay in the quarters all day and as the people came walking around we'd get under the bed and hide ourselves, you know, so that nobody'd take us away.'

. . . .

'All Aboriginal people were Wards of the State and that was the law. A Magistrate only had to sign a piece of paper and people could just say, "Well, okay, you're going to Moore River", and you'd be sent accordingly. Hundreds were uprooted like this and sent there. And of course this not only happened in the south, it happened all over Western Australia. If these people became an embarrassment to their fathers who were white—they were half-caste children—they were just bundled up and all sent down to Moore River at the stroke of a pen or at the whim of the local Police Sergeant, as a matter of fact.'

. . . .

'I was part of the settlement like a lot of Aborigines were part of the settlement. Their mothers and fathers were taken away from up the north—my mother came from the Murchison country. They were still bringing people in from the north and the south in the 'forties. They lined them up between the office and the boys' dormitory. Now a lot of these fellers couldn't talk English and the Superintendent'd have a book in his hand and he'd have the black tracker standing alongside of him who didn't understand [enough] to read and write or even couldn't count, and they'd walk along the line and they'd say to a bloke, "What's your name?" If one feller couldn't talk, [the Superintendent would say] "Why, he doesn't know his name", and they'd put him down as "Friday". Or if he said something in Australian language—that's Aborigine language—they'd call him "Wheelbarrow", and the next one "Horseshoe Tommy" or "Billycan Bill".'

. . . .

Jack Davis has very vivid memories of an old man who was called Skipper.

'Of course, me being a boy of fourteen, anybody who had a long white beard was old; but, looking back, I think he would have probably been about fifty years of age. His wife was blind—an enormously big woman—her name was Nora. She was completely blind and he was, I would have said, eighty per cent blind and they lived together. And one of the most vivid experiences of my life was to sit down with those two at night and hear [them] sing. I have never heard anything in my life since, or before, that could rival those two in power of voice. Everybody in the whole community used to stop when those two used to sing their Aboriginal songs at the top of their voices. The power and the range and the tremolo, it was just absolutely amazing; it was just marvellous. They were singing about their country which they knew they were never going to see again. It was all they were singing about—their country—which was the Kimberleys.'

But some Aborigines did make it back to their own country. Margaret Morgan and Reggie Johnston, together with Alice Nannup, recall the escape of fifteen people in 1926. They'd been rounded up by the police in Laverton to be sent to Mogumber, a thousand kilometres away. Margaret Morgan's father had gone down to the police station to find out what had happened to them.

'He didn't know then—all he saw was that when he went down to the train he saw this cattle truck with a little notice outside of the truck "Fifteen Niggers for Mogumber". They made a big crate on the truck and they piled in these poor old people, you know, and there was a blind man there, and one had a broken leg. There were women and children and other men as well and they were all brought to Mogumber. They were very shy, couldn't speak English, some of them. They just lived on the compound and every now and again they'd move camp, just kept on moving camp. Each night they'd move to another place, and one night they made the escape and went back home. But they had to get over the river and they got over it by seeing a big tree and using it as a bridge and dropping on the other side. Now, they had old people with them and they had a blind man with them. Wowija was a strong young fellow, they tell me, and he helped get these old and blind across.'

'They were in fear when they were travelling. They couldn't light a flame because they were frightened the police would follow them up and put them in jail.'

'The trackers were told to get after them and look for them, but not one of them were game because they didn't belong to that tribe and they would have been killed themselves. In the morning they woke up and they looked to see where they were going to go. They looked at the sun and they worked out where they reckoned home was.'

. . . .

'They could read the stars—they could find a star like the Seven Sisters, they know that up north, so they followed the Seven Sisters . . .'

'And on the way they left an old man who knew he was going to peter out, so they left him with his fire and never saw him again. The blind one, he was holding them up so they just left him in a paddock and that's the most incredible story of all, because they said he sat in the paddock and he yelled for all he was worth and a farmer heard him, took him home to Yalgoo, of all places, which is further north, and when he got there sent the message around that he had this old man and did anyone know who he belonged to.'

'They took him to Mount Magnet then and found out his sister was there, so the sister had to walk all the way from Magnet through Sandstone, about 800 kilometres she had to walk.'

'They had a big long stick and they led this fellow home.'

'They were glad when they went back. Some of their old people died when they returned but many of them never returned.'

. . . .

Those who did completed their thousand kilometre walk back to Laverton in just fourteen days.

Perhaps those most affected by the policy which gave rise to Moore River were children. As Sister Eileen recalls:

'There was a policy of "drift". People were put there to be out of sight and out of mind. The children particularly were sent there for so-called education and protection.'

But they had to endure conditions which Sister Eileen also recalls:

'The sanitation in the dormitories was absolutely appalling. The staff went in and they'd say, "I'll have to have a cigarette before I go in". There were no toilets there at all, there were just sanitary buckets which were emptied each morning. They were very dimly lit, cyclone beds, no sheets of course, blankets, bug-ridden. When anybody special was coming to the settlement, we had a stock of sheets which were put on the beds so that if anybody wanted to go into the dormitories to have a look they got the impression that the children always had sheets on their beds. The compound was lined with pine trees, or fir trees, and when anybody special was coming they were whitewashed all the way up the trunks, the camp people were. told to tidy up, get the rubbish out of the way so it gave the impression that the place was reasonably clean.'

. . . .

'In Moore River Aboriginal Settlement there was the main compound and then you'd go further down the river to the camps. You'd have camps down there—you'd have two people picked out to cook, that'd be a man and wife. There'd be breakfast, dinner and supper. Each time the meals were ready the old tin would be rattled or the iron would be hammered out and everybody would come running out of their camps with their billycans, pots, to get a bit of soup or something.'

. . . .

'The children were housed in dormitories, dreadful buildings, long, very ill-lit, closed in with wire mesh. They had to be locked in at night-time for safety and protection. If anybody had to go into a dormitory at night-time, the lights were outside and we just switched on as we went in. But once the children were locked up in the dormitory there was no supervision whatever.'

. . . .

'The worst thing about it was, when you went into the dormitory at night you didn't know whether you were going to come out in one piece or not. The girls would chew up things that weren't true and they'd come and face you and want to fight you—they were bored, nothing to do, I suppose.'

. . . .

'They had to make clothes for the ones at the Mission and they needed girls, so they took me out of school. They took about four of us out of school, and took us down to the sewing room. They had a lady there doing the cutting out, and all the girls had machines and were sewing. We had to get these clothes done.'

'Do you know what we used to get paid every Saturday morning? A bar of chocolate! No money, we never saw money.'

'They didn't want to give us a formal education. Mr Neville said one day, "As long as they can count money and write their name, that is all they need". What sort of an education is that?'

. . . .

'A lot of us boys were interested in schooling but they couldn't teach us any schooling. They never had the teachers, never had the paper, never had the pencils, never had the space.'

. . . .

'The teachers were not Education Department teachers. They were not trained teachers. We had two teachers most of the time, about 150 children, and the highest grade that they would have achieved would have been Grade 4. There was a constant turnover of teachers and the children didn't complete the normal education. I felt that a lot of the children there and a lot of the people had so much good in them and so much could have been done if they were given the right opportunities.'

. . . .

'What caused me to be so bitter about it all was that when I came down south we were under the impression we would go to school then go back home. But when we were shoved into the Mission, well, that was the end of everything.'

. . . .

'There was no incentive whatsoever for employment or doing anything. In fact, it was said to me by some people who came and looked at the settlement that what should have been written across the place was "Abandon hope, all ye who enter here".'

'A lot of the girls used to want to get away from there. Some of them jumped a train to go to Perth.

'They used to take them back and lock them up but they'd do it again. They were the ones who couldn't settle, or just wanted to get out and see what life was all about, I suppose.'

. . . .

'If the girls ran away they were tracked by the trackers, apprehended and brought back again and locked up in the place we called "the boob", which was a small, galvanised iron building with no proper facilities either for washing or for toilet. Their food was taken to them. They had no exercise and they were left there for varying periods according to their misdemeanours.'

. . . .

'One of the buildings was introduced to me (Stanley Middleton) as being "the boob". I knew, because I'm a country Queenslander, what was meant by "boob"—it was prison. I said, "What have you got this for?" "Oh", he said, "we lock them up." I said, "Why?" "Oh", he said, "if they've done anything wrong, you know, fighting or doing anything they shouldn't, we put them in here for the night." But I said, "On what authority?" "Oh," he said, "I'm the Superintendent." '

. . . .

'They went as far as tarring and feathering a bloke here, and he got it through talking to girls and stealing cigarettes. He tarred and feathered him, the Superintendent.

'He had to run all the way down there in no clothes down to the bottom and they put hot water on to get the tar off him.'

. . . .

'The way that these places were conducted would depend very largely on the characters and the attitudes of the white staff. Not all of these were the ideal people to have in charge of institutions of that nature.'

. . . .

'We would get rejects from the Police Force, people who'd retired from the Police Force. The Superintendent who was there when I was there was a Boer War veteran, very militaristic in his style, very much suited for Moore River Settlement—I think the type of person who would have been suitable to Hitler in Nazi Germany.'

. . . .

'I think the wrong type of people were put there. At one stage they put migrants there—Polish and I think Russians. They were brought up to be staff, cooking and so on, and nobody understood them, nobody understood their ways, they'd never had anything to do with Aboriginals before, they were new to the country.'

. . . .

Joy Mort joined the staff at Moore River as a nursing assistant in 1948:

'I was out of work. I used to read the daily papers to look for a job, a suitable kind of job. I wasn't trained in anything in particular. I looked up the newspaper [and saw] "Nursing Assistant wanted by Native Affairs" so I applied. I wasn't asked for any qualifications, just "When would you like to start?" "As soon as possible" I said. "Can you be on the train tomorrow? You'll escort an Aboriginal woman up with you." We got on the train together and went up there. There were no qualifications wanted.'

'Maybe the staff wasn't exactly right—I mean, I was brought in more or less off the road, untrained, unskilled in any particular way, and put in positions where I had to try and teach them. Now, the sewing room was one example. I was in charge of the sewing room, but some women, like one Aboriginal woman, could run rings around me. But I was more or less there to supervise.'

. . . .

'The buildings were getting run down, equipment was run down, bedding and things like that should have been thrown to the dump years before. The mattresses were appalling, they really were.'

. . . .

Stanley Middleton closed down Moore River in August 1951. It was the end of an era and the beginning of a new policy towards Aboriginal Australians:

'It was very obvious to me that it was very badly run down, very badly managed and something needed to be done about it as a matter of urgency. I felt that I could in no way hold myself responsible for the maintenance of a place like that.'

But Moore River and other places like it have made their mark on those who'd already been through them.

'It made us very weak, and it made a lot of us very strong.'

'The sad thing is that, instead of their reacting in anger and hatred, they in effect didn't react at all. They became thoroughly depressed and apathetic.'

. . . .

'I think everyone was completely ignorant how to handle the situation. Aboriginal people didn't know how to handle it and certainly the government didn't know how to handle it. They were suddenly stuck with a race of people who was here, who was not supposed to be here.'

. . . .

'The effect of keeping full-blood people down had failed and all of a sudden the half-caste population was there on their doorstep, and most of them were related to *them*, the whites, and therefore they didn't know how to handle it.'

. . . .

'I suppose they thought they were doing good, but I don't know whether they were or not. They just didn't want half-castes to be mixed up with the full-bloods and they wanted to get them away on that account, I think.'

. . . .

'I used to love my father and he was white, you know, but I loved my mother just the same. They were just equal, there was no difference between them. They were both human beings.'

. . . .

Sister Eileen, with the last word on Moore River Aboriginal Settlement:

'They were a very fine race of people, very deprived, with very little hope. They regarded Moore River as a punishment. They just had no opportunity at all; once they were at Mogumber, they were just out of sight and out of mind.'

Anybody Could Afford Us

'We were servants—trained as servants. Just cheap labour for middle-class white people who could afford us—for that matter anybody could afford us, I suppose.'

· ·

Like many others, Iris Clayton was taken from her family in the 1930s to spend most of her childhood in a home for Aboriginal girls—the Cootamundra Girls' Home in New South Wales.

· · · ·

'My parents separated and then the Welfare came out and there were six of us taken. The eldest six—there were nine in my family altogether—were just put on a train and taken off to Cootamundra [Girls' Home]. The whole of Wattle Hill was very upset at the time. We had people crying all the week before we went. And we got to Cootamundra—my mother took me there—and she said, "It's just going to be a holiday. It'll only be for a little while and we'll all be back together". But we found out, of course, rather differently, that it wasn't.

'Matron met us down at the railway station and when we got up to the Home the first thing she did was shove us all in a hot bath and cut our hair off—we had very long hair those days—and scrub us until we were practically pink. And then they checked the bathtub after us to see if there was any ring around it. It was incredible, really. It was a good thing my mother bathed us in the morning, though, before we went. But that was the introduction to Cootamundra—bath and haircut.

'We all went to Cootamundra together but then the two

74

boys were sent up to Kinsella. I never saw them again until I was fifteen or sixteen.

'You missed your grandmothers. I was very, very close to my grandmothers and I missed them terribly, and it was very, very hard to settle down there for a while. We did write, backwards and forwards, but Matron always read our mail, so if there was anything there that she didn't think should be there she'd cross it out. If somebody died, or if your mother was coming to see you and if she was going to get in touch with Matron, well, that was crossed out, and Matron would say "I crossed that out because your mother was going to come and see you, but I don't think it's allowable at this stage". So you weren't allowed to see your parents, either.

'You felt cut off. Really cut right off. They tried to wipe out your whole family background in one hit. You were kept away from all relationships like that.'

. . . .

'There is everywhere the common experience of Aboriginal children being taken away from their families and the splitting up of families—forced removals of groups and families to different stations, reserves and so on. Aboriginal girls taken away from their families were forced into domestic service for 1/6d a week in the 1930s until they were eighteen years of age.'

. . . .

'You were trained from the time you got there. You got up at half-six in the morning. The first thing you did was strip your bed, or the staff stripped it for you. You bed was made under supervision. They used to bounce a sixpence on it. If it wasn't made properly, your bed would be stripped down again and you'd have to remake it until it was done properly.

'The girls did some homework. That was just to keep them in school, I think. High education wasn't encouraged.

'I've only known about three or four girls that went through Cootamundra that came out with an Intermediate Certificate. Keep them dumb and black, that was the whole idea, because no white person wanted an educated blackfeller working for them, telling them what to do. We were sort of brought up with white outlooks. We were never taught black things. If we used Aboriginal words at the Home we were punished, or if we sort of spoke "black" we were punished. There was a family there who had a real Aboriginal accent and Matron often checked them—you know, "I'll have none of that black talk here", which was a shame because they were lovely girls and they had a true, natural sort of real lovely, flowing Aboriginal accent and it was just taught out of them.

'It's a sad story really, because there were suicides, there was prostitution, there was alcoholism—a lot of girls died from cirrhosis of the liver through being alcoholics. And a hell of a lot committed suicide. They just couldn't cope with being black but not being black.'

· · · ·

'The man that my mother was living with, he was a well sinker, and the police came out and picked us up, so she was picked up and we came in to Waroona. We were there for a couple of days till the train was coming to Perth, so they put us on the train. And someone else met us in Perth. We didn't know where we were going or anything—well, I didn't— and we came to Mogumber by train. We were scared because everybody was staring at you and wanting to know where you came from, and some of them were nasty and some of them weren't. I didn't know where my brothers were going and I had two cousins go at the same time, and I was sort of out on a limb—I just had to make the best of it. Didn't know where they were going or anything.'

· · · ·

'There are many people in the situation where they don't know who their family is or where they come from. So that sense of not belonging to anybody would be even more traumatic. And I think that this even permeated through to people that were adopted out. Later on, even twenty or thirty years later into their lives, they are saying that they want to find out who their mother and father are.'

· · · ·

'My mother got taken away when I was a little feller, and married. She couldn't take me with her. This was the part that really hurt me. I was a fair Aboriginal child, born on a reserve, so therefore I'm under the government.'

· · · ·

'You were policed by black policemen, black trackers. You were locked up in the compound at 6 o'clock and you were let out at 6 o'clock in the morning. You had to go out to work. You weren't paid for your labour—the labour was really not hard work, I can't say they were masters that stood over us, but it was this policing you all your time, all your behaviour, your patterns and everything, the way you behaved. If you had a sore on your arm someone would grab you—somebody in authority—and pull your arm up. "You get up to the hospital, go on". So you went up to the hospital and they dressed it. They were looking after you but you had no independence.'

· · · ·

'We worked. When the bell rang you had to toe the line and be there. They had a big kitchen where everybody went for their meals. We got one meal a day, greasy stew, what was left over from the trotters and the guts, and they boiled this all up with an onion and potato. They had a big copper for a boiler to boil the stew. You got that meal with a slice of bread and fat. If you were lucky enough you'd pinch another slice and put it down your shirt. Now, that meal had to last you all day. You got to go down the river—we had a river in the Settlement—and we caught little fish, little yabbies, all that sort of thing. We ate what crawled, even bob-tail goanna and beehive bird. We ate every bird, every fish, that crawled, walked or flew or swam.'

. . . .

'Cootamundra helped me in the white society but it didn't help me with the black society. I mean, you went back to your parents but they were complete strangers. All your relations were. Everybody was just a stranger to each other. There were nine of us in the family but six of us were taken. Now there's a bit of a gap between the ones that were taken to Cootamundra and the ones that were left home with Mum. There's not that closeness between us. It's really affected the whole family, the family structure.'

. . . .

'I don't know whether words can explain the sense of belonging that one can have to a family that you've never known. Just having people that are really flesh and blood. You always know where you come from, where your roots are.'

. . . .

'I had my mother to think of. She finished up going back to the Mogumber Mission to look after the girls in the dormitory and I was working [with a man called Jim] when she passed away. I was a carpenter, we were making coffins and all that. He said to me "You'd better go up there and measure Clara Leyland". I said, "That's my mother". You see, you didn't know, you were away from them. Well, I just stopped and I looked at him and he said, "Well, maybe you'd better go home, go back down to the camp".'

. . . .

'You were given this little book when you first went to work. You left school and then you got up one morning and Matron would say to you, "You're going to work today". You didn't know anything about it beforehand, right? So you rushed around—the staff packed your bags the night before—to say your goodbyes to your family. You didn't know when the hell you were going to see them again, your sisters and brothers, and that was rough. That was terrible. Anyway, you were scrubbed up and chucked in the car and half-way to Canberra I said to Matron, "Where am I going?" She said, "Oh, Canberra". That was half-way here—I was half-way here and she told me I was coming to Canberra.

'And then you were given this book. "Now", she said, "this is your booklet. These are your wages—you've got to sign that each week." There was 2/6d for me, that's 25c today, 10/- had to go into my bank account. She said, "Make sure you sign that". That was the first time I'd ever handled money. I was fifteen years old and I was given 2/6d a week, you know. And I thought, "Whoopee, I'm rich; I'm going to save up and buy a house so I can get my brothers and sisters out of the home". On 10/- a week I had high dreams. Of course, that didn't come about. I still don't own a house, or land.'

. . . .

'Domestic work, that's all we could do, but we weren't paid that much in those days. Sometimes I thought well, things could be better for us than just working as maids and waiting on white people and that sort of thing.'

. . . .

79

'I was all right. I was treated all right but a lot of girls weren't. They were bashed. Some of the girls went out on to the stations—they ended up being pregnant by the station owners themselves. Then those girls that were made pregnant out on the stations were sent to Sydney, to Parramatta Girls' Home, for being uncontrollable. And then their kids were either adopted out or they were given abortions, and these are the ones that went into prostitution.'

. . . .

'We were servants, trained as servants, just cheap labour for middle-class white people who could afford us. For that matter anybody could afford us, I suppose.'

. . . .

'We weren't taught anything about money—not a thing. We didn't even know what an award meant. The only "award" we knew was "a ward of the state", not award in wages.'

. . . .

'The whole pastoral industry has been developed on the back of Aboriginal people, Aboriginal labour, this being very cheap labour then.'

. . . .

'They talk about the way the white feller went up there and how he worked and what he did to get his farm to where it is now, and that's not true at all. I remember my old man used to do a lot of cutting down with axe and he cleared a lot of property, and when he finished clearing the five or six hundred acres, or whatever it was, the boss came to him after he'd finished it and said, "Well, you've done a good job," he said, "and here's your pay". He handed him an old shot-gun and a sack of flour.'

80

'We lived in a two-bedroom camp the old man built himself. It didn't have any flooring or things like that. We worked for a farmer who lived in a six- or eight-bedroom house. We just accepted that, that we should be living in those conditions. There was no question about it. We didn't have any running water at all. We used to cart all our water. In the winter it was just impossible to have showers or things like that and in the morning Mum used to go outside and make a big fire and that's how she used to cook our breakfast. If it was raining we had to try and have our breakfast in between showers without getting wet. We lived in those conditions for at least ten years.

'There was a white bloke who, because his farm was getting bigger, employed a white bloke. He had one child and his wife and himself, and before he got there he built him a new house. It was a three-bedroom house and it was brand new and that's where he went to live, and we were still living in our camp. He didn't ask us if we wanted anything else. He knew how we lived and he accepted that.'

· · · ·

'The whole opening up of the rural industry, particularly the farming industry, was done with the knowledge of Aboriginal people who showed the farmers (in the early days the settlers) where the best areas of land were.'

· · · ·

'We didn't get the things the other shearers got, like lunch and, maybe, living in and showers and things like that. I remember one day it was lunch time and we knocked off for lunch. We were standing outside and all of a sudden a guy came over with my lunch and my old man's lunch in his hand and he said, "You can have it here on the woodheap if you want but you can't eat inside". Of course, we told him, that's

81

his sheep, that's his shearing. If we weren't good enough to eat at his table we weren't good enough to shear his sheep. Well, he went hysterical and he said, "Oh, I didn't mean to say it. I didn't know it would affect you". He was talking to a human being, and, when I think about it, it seems to me that he didn't know that.'

. . . .

'Even as recently as thirty or forty years ago, Aboriginal people were treated to that degree of being aliens within their own country and being made to feel inferior.'

. . . .

'In those days and, to a lesser extent, even today, the way of Aboriginal living was determined by high authorities, by the government of the day and, certainly, by Native Welfare. We couldn't do anything unless it was with the express approval of those sorts of parties. We knew we couldn't really go into town all that often without feeling guilty and that the police had total and sole authority over our lives in regards to where we were and what we were doing.'

. . . .

'The whole world speaks about laws, apartheid in South Africa, but we had those laws long before South Africa did, in Australia, to keep Aboriginal people down. It wasn't set up to keep Aboriginal people down, it was set up because they believed in the 'dying pillow' policy. They thought Aboriginal people were dying out. Well, they *were* dying out back in the 1870s and the 1880s and the 1890s, but they didn't realise that the Aboriginal population was growing, especially the part-Aboriginal population, and these 'dying pillow' policies were still carried out, such as laws where you had to leave the town at 6 o'clock for your own protection. But those laws were still in existence in the 'thirties when they no longer applied but nobody worried about changing them. So those laws to us were oppression. If you were told to get home at 6 o'clock and you didn't do it, well, you were slammed in jail.'

. . . .

'There were places where it was "Out at 6 . . . out at 6, get your tucker by 6 and out". Now, if [the police] caught you there they'd rough you up, perhaps throw you in.'

. . . .

'Well, we didn't have any of this legal aid, we had nothing. Nothing. If they said "shift", you shifted.'

. . . .

'The reason Aboriginals became fringe dwellers is plain to see. The fringe-living life was created and caused by the coming of the white public in general and its existence today in Australia. They had to take up land and their progress forced Aboriginal people to become fringe dwellers on the edges of town. That progress automatically pushed on from back there in the yesterdays of the past right to the present, where Aboriginal people are situated now, living in vacant blocks, under bridges and whatever.'

. . . .

'We were actually fringe dwellers. I put myself down as a scrounger. All I lived on was selling bottles, scrap metal, anything I could sell. Prop sticks, cobweb brooms, we used to make them for the ladies. The main thing then was props, selling prop sticks and, mind you, that was hard. My dad used to carry six forky sticks, six of them, and I'd only carry two. I'd get rid of mine and he'd say "Oh, well, take some tucker home to Mum".'

. . . .

'I remember my father cutting the sticks off the peppermint tree to make camps and making stick beds and putting pepper tree leaves down for mattresses, and always continuously going out and walking the streets and asking people for old clothes and things and selling cool drink bottles and things, and asking for stale bread and things like that.

'That fringe-dwelling lifestyle of Aboriginal people was in the 'thirties, mid-thirties, coming right the way up 'till now.'

. . . .

'The history of the Second World War in the Torres Straits, or in North Queensland or in New South Wales is quite different. In New South Wales, for instance, the Aboriginal leadership went to fight for Australia, believing that that would be a step to citizenship. How disappointed they were!'

. . . .

'Just imagine how traumatic it must have been for returned servicemen who'd gone away, fought and risked their lives to come back to a country and have to fall into the requirements of getting an Act [of Parliament passed] so that they could walk the streets that they had so gallantly gone overseas to defend.'

. . . .

'When I got discharged out of the Army we went up to Leonora and all our friends were there, but I couldn't walk in with them to have a drink, you know. You couldn't get a decent house to live in. Even the police would check on you after 6 o'clock at night. If you got caught on the street the policeman would run you in, you understand that? I ended up fighting against it. I said, "I went away and fought for my country, why should I come back as a migrant? I was bred and born here".'

'Aboriginal people enlisted in the armed forces and went across overseas. Some died for the cause in that respect and that's something that's not recognised as such, as being one of the positive contributions that Aboriginal people have made to this country. I know of many, many instances where returned Aboriginal servicemen came back to this country, after fighting for the country, and were not accepted as equals. Aboriginal people weren't afforded the same opportunities in relation to farm allotments as a lot of returned servicemen.'

. . . .

'Dad was a returned soldier. He was allocated a block of land, twelve acres and a house. It had no electricity, no running water or anything. There was a well that was dug by my parents. There was a soak at the other end of the paddock from which we had to draw water and, in fact, that was one of our duties. We had a bucket, and us kids used to go up the other end of the paddock and draw the water and lump it back to the house. In fact, I remember the only baths we had was every Sunday because of that difficulty.'

. . . .

'In 1955 it still wasn't compulsory for Aboriginal people to go to school. In previous years it wasn't encouraged, and the fact that Aboriginal people now are involved themselves in attempting to address the many issues in the experiences of Aboriginal people is something that no European, no matter how involved or how committed they are to Aboriginal issues, will ever understand or appreciate, simply because they've never had the experience of being an Aboriginal in Australia.'

. . . .

'It was a difficult experience for most of us Aboriginal kids. We weren't allowed to live inside the town limits, and that's the reason why that Reserve was two miles outside of town. We were virtually betwixt and between, I guess.

'You had farm children going to school and they had transport—they had school buses—and you had the town children living within the township going to the school, and you had us, the Aboriginal children, walking to school, often without proper school uniform, nine times out of ten without any shoes on your feet, tramping the couple of miles to school and then fronting up to the teachers, sometimes late, sometimes without breakfast. All those sorts of problems often were difficult for teachers and other of the non-Aboriginal schoolchildren to understand.'

. . . .

'We used to cop the cane, I guess, three or four times as much as any ordinary white European would, and when we came to school we came to school as a disadvantaged people. We never had the kind of things that it was our right to have. We weren't dressed like the ordinary schoolkids were. I remember going to school without even any pair of shoes. I used to have a pair of football boots and that's what I had on and I wasn't allowed to wear them inside because they'd scrape the floor, they told me because of the springs on my boots. So I never used to wear them till every Friday, and every other day I used to go to school with no shoes on because we couldn't afford another pair of shoes for myself. I used to have to try and sit down to study and my feet were cold and I was thinking about what I was going to have for lunch and things like that. Those were the disadvantages, I think, that the average Aboriginal people would have experienced.'

. . . .

'I can remember one incident at school where one of my best friends, in fact, was a non-Aboriginal fellow. He was a farmer, or his father was a farmer and quite rich. But he did invite me out to his house on a weekend and I then immediately thought of things like pyjamas, which I didn't have, and toothpaste and toothbrushes, which I didn't have—no Aboriginal kid did—and underpants and singlets and so on. So I went home with that request for Mum and Dad to see if they could get those things together with a small case. We got all those things together on the Friday when I took the case to school. This best friend of mine then told me that I couldn't go out there because his sister, who was a model in the city, was coming back and he'd told his parents and his sister about me coming out there, an Aboriginal kid. I knew my friend very well and I knew that he had problems with explaining that to his parents and so on—they couldn't accept that an Aboriginal person was going to go out there on the farm. I mean, that really made me feel low. I didn't ever get out there to see him, or his farm.'

. . . .

'The history that we were taught was history about English history. The curriculum for all children, including Aboriginal, was that it taught about English history and the early days of colonisation. The only reference to Aboriginal history was the fact that there were Aborigines and they were savages and they had spears and hunted kangaroos. The fact that we had to live outside of town and all those other things like not having the correct uniform reinforced the idea that we were second-class citizens, and the fact that the history books made reference to savages and that we carried spears and that we killed white settlers, again reinforced the feeling that we were inferior.'

. . . .

'Aboriginal parents see their children coming home from school and regurgitating the school curricula version of Australian history, which still today teaches our children that Captain Cook discovered Australia. All that view is anathema to Aboriginal people. We've been here since time immemorial and we want our children to understand what it means to be Aboriginal, and that is that our children must know who they are.'

Shorty O'Neill

'That call was going out for "my sisters, Judith, Maureen and Jennifer and Sheddah, all out at Yunilgie Outstation", and it's coming your way from your brother Norman.

'This is your Aboriginal family radio right here in the centre of Aboriginal country and this is a special program for that part of our family who got locked up.'

· ·

Shorty O'Neill broadcasts over CAAMA Radio in Alice Springs, presenting a special program for Aboriginal prisoners, playing their requests and putting them in touch with family and friends outside. The prison experience is familiar to many Aboriginal people and it was very real for Shorty O'Neill in the early part of his life.

· · · ·

'I grew up on Palm Island, which is one of the concentration camps for Aboriginal people in North Queensland. I grew up under the Queensland Aboriginal Act and I guess I started work when I was about ten and a half years of age on a cattle property. I still haven't been paid for that work.

'The Queensland Protection Act was used as a basis for the South African Apartheid Act in 1910 when South Africa became independent from Britain. They sent their experts to Australia, and to Queensland specifically, [to study] the Queensland Aboriginal Act and they took it back to South Africa and implemented it. That became the Protection Act in South Africa. But later on, in 1948, when the present Afrikan Government came into power, they sent their experts back to Queensland again to see how the Act had been developed, and they must have fallen so much in love with it that they took it back and implemented it in full. That laid the basis for the South African apartheid system as it's now known today.

'On Palm Island the community was run by bells. We used to have to get up by a bell and go to work by a bell, and if we didn't follow the bell system, well, then we'd be locked up for a couple of months. But worst of all was the bell at night, when they'd ring a bell about half past eight and everybody would have to be home in bed and all the whites had to be off in houses. It was total control of the community of Aboriginal people.

'On the Reserve everybody was given a job and we were given rations and if you didn't work you were locked up. But what was happening was that the kids on Palm Island and, I believe, every reserve in the country at that time, were trained in the cattle industry, or the boys were trained in the cattle industry, and the girls were trained as domestic slaves. And we were sent out to pastoral properties when they believed that we were old enough to work. We were never paid for those jobs. In fact, Aboriginal stockmen in Australia didn't get the award wage until 1968. It was only in the early '60s when we got a little bit of pay, but that was taken off us and put into a bank account and managed; you had to go along to a policeman or to the Native Protector, who was usually a policeman, and ask him if you could draw your own money out of your own bank account, and there was always a very big hassle to do that.

'You weren't allowed to travel at any time. You had to have a travel pass. If you didn't—if you were an Aboriginal person and the police picked you up and you didn't have a travel pass or you didn't have what they called an exemption pass—then you were sent back to the Mission very quickly.

'I'm a little bit lighter skinned than most people and I stuck it out on the station for about nine months then I took off and got interstate. It's not so noticeable that I'm Aboriginal so I got out of the Queensland Act. And I guess from then on I got into a bit of strife with the police. I spent a number of years in jail and that was mainly for assault and things like that.

'I was sticking up for my own rights and the rights of my fellow Aboriginal relations. The first time I ever went to jail was for assaulting a police officer: I broke his jaw in two places. I wasn't quite twelve years of age, and it was because he was hassling one of my cousins. When he walked away I got into him, which was a bit of a joke but it wasn't a big joke for me because I ended up in jail for quite some time. And I continued to do that for . . . I guess, up until the time I was about twenty-six. I was in and out of jail most of my life, and it was mainly for assaulting police officers or other people who were blatantly showing racism or being oppressive to either myself or other members of my family. That was something that I've never been able to put up with. When I got about the age of twenty-six I learnt that, well, you don't do it by assaulting people, you can do it better with your mouth. So I guess that's put me onto the road where I'm at now.

'I was just getting sick and tired of being in jail and wasting my life inside. I realised that I had to cool it a bit or I'd end up being permanently in jail. I continually had to restrain myself from doing those types of things. I became involved in community organisations and I started to write newspapers and became a newspaper editor—before I learnt to read and write. I was co-director of the Palm Island Adult Education Centre. I guess I was one of the few people who showed a lot of interest back at home, and at that stage I couldn't read or write.

'When you look at it, you see that Bob Hawke or any Prime Minister in this country doesn't do all the work himself, he hires an expert to do it. I decided that if I was going to be an editor of a newspaper and I couldn't read or write, I'd hire a person who could, an expert. A lot of the articles I wrote I would put down on cassette tape and the secretary I had would take them off that tape and then read them back to me. If it was other articles that needed to go into the newspaper, then she'd read them to me and I'd tell her to take something or other out if it needed to go out. But I got sick of that and thought, well, this is a waste of time, why don't you learn to read and write? And I did, very quickly, once I set my mind to it.'

. . . .

After working in newspapers and publishing, Shorty O'Neill travelled overseas, furthering the cause of his own people and learning about other minority groups in Europe and North America. On his return to Australia he was attracted by the challenge that radio offered, especially in Central Australia, where CAAMA Radio had just begun to broadcast.

'I think it was a normal step for an Aboriginal educator to get from newspapers and other things into radio, and the one organisation in Alice Springs that I was very confident with and I saw was going places was CAAMA. I used to come up and do things on the side so we sat down and talked and said "Well, it'd be good to have a weekly hour political show or give a national view". I guess I started off doing an hour a week and then, with CAAMA expanding the way it was and with me being as enthusiastic as I am about things that I get involved in, I ended up doing whole heaps of shows and other things. But mainly I guess I'm a broadcaster. I like doing radio because its the medium for an educator. I like the possibilities that it can have for our people.'

. . . .

Shorty O'Neill

You've got one particular program that reaches prisoners which you run on CAAMA Radio. What gave you the idea to do that?

'If you look at the jail population all over Australia, depending on whoever you talk to, [it's] one and a half per cent of the population, yet the permanent jail population of Aboriginal people is forty-five per cent at any given time. In fact, a report four or five years ago said that Aboriginal people were the most imprisoned of any minority group anywhere in the world, and if you look at the local prison, something like ninety per cent of the prisoners are Aboriginal.

'We always get a lot of requests—cheerio calls from people outside of the prison to prisoners, and we've had to fit them in to any program [we could]. But when we extended our hours one of the things that everybody agreed with was that we should have a specific prison program. So I was given the task of putting that program together. It's one of the programs I really enjoy doing. I don't see that as a job. This is a program that I particularly enjoy because I don't think there are many Aboriginal people around who could say that they've never been in prison. The majority of us have been in prison.

'The program gets all the cheerio calls out and I get heaps of people coming out of prison and telling me [that] it's really great, it helps them through their terms in prison, it gives them an interest while they're in there. I'm not as happy with it as I could be. It's mainly a request program. I've tried to do other things with it [but] it's going to take a long time to do that.

'We've had a lot of obstacles put in our way [with the] program, particularly with the prison authorities, who at one stage completely stopped requests coming out of the prison. We had to do a three months' lobbying campaign and activist campaign around the whole prison show to get requests from the prison.

'[The authorities] believed that they may give escape plans in code over a request program, which was a bit far out. But I was talking to the Department of Correctional Services and I got the local Unions involved and we went and talked our way through it. It took about three months [to be] able to get requests from the prison, which is important because it *is* a program for the prisoners. Since then we've had numerous problems. I've visited the prison quite regularly and have been told by prisoners that they've found a lot of their requests in the rubbish bins inside the prisons. A lot of the requests are held up by the authorities within the jail. But generally speaking it's starting to go well and the authorities are now coming to see that the program is, in fact, an asset to them because it keeps the prisoners much happier and it gets rid of a lot of the problems that could be there.

'I guess I could have [made this program even if I hadn't experienced prison.] There are people here who haven't been inside and who have done the program when I'm away. I think probably my experience in the prisons has helped. There are some other things I think that I'd like to [do] and they're things on the education side, trying to help educate prisoners who are inside. And there are a lot of things we could do in that area. We just have to get it together.'

. . . .

'Hello! I'm Shorty and this is our special program for all our friends and relations who've been taken off us for a short time, not too long we hope. Let all you mob know that we're still thinking about you out here and hope it won't be too long before you're back out here with us once again. And it's for you mob to get your choice of music and any messages you want passed on or anything else you want done with the program. Think about that. There's probably a whole heap of things we could do with this program.'

94

Paddy Roe

'I was very lucky, because I learned both sides. I learned European ways—I can run the station, sheep station, cattle station; on the European side, station jobs, that's my game. I was a station-hand. But on the other side, that's my people's side, I come in handy on their side, too, because I can carry their culture.'

. . . .

Paddy Roe was born in 1912 on the Roebuck Plain, near Broome, country he often re-visits and which is spiritually very important to him. His natural father was white but his tribal father was a full-blood Aborigine. He grew up between two worlds, traditional Aboriginal society and the white man's world of station work on the northwest cattle and sheep stations:

'When I was born on the station, that was a sheep station, I was born in the bush. So, when my mother brought me out after she was in the hospital away from the people, a lot of people saw I was a different colour, a lighter colour.

'My tribe didn't like to see me with that colour because I was the only one in the tribe with that colour. They were going to kill me. But my father, my full-blood father, he was a big man in the tribe, a big boss. (My name should have been Buru instead of Roe.) My father made a big meeting with the people, my people, his people too, and he talked. "This little boy, we all know he's got different colour, but" he said, "we're going to leave him, let him grow because sooner or later" he said, in the language, "there's going to be a lot more of this [lighter people] come up. So, this boy, we've got to leave him. He might come in handy to us." And that's true, too. I did come handy to them.'

95

Paddy's parents were traditional Aboriginal people but they also worked for white pastoralists.

'My father used to work in the station. He used to do any sort of job, fencing, windmill, tanks, stock work—well, we only had sheep those days—mustering sheep, droving.'

Was your father paid for that work?

'No, no money, only tucker. Just tucker to live on, bread and meat and tea, that's all. No other tucker.'

Did your father get tucker from the traditional ways? Did he go and get tucker from the bush as well?

'Yes, they got their tucker from the bush too.'

What did your mother do? Was she living on the station as well?

'She used to cook, wash up plates, laundry, housekeeping . . . look after the house for the boss.'

If Paddy owes his survival to his tribal father, he owes his tribal education to his mother. If it had not been for her vigilance he would have been taken from his family and community and sent to Mission School for a European-style education. This was a typical prospect for part-Aboriginal children in the 1920s and 1930s.

'The policemen used to take all the children away, you know, and my mother saved [me from] that. I was the only child with this colour in all my tribe so my mother said, "Oh, this is no good", because my mother saw these children being taken by the police, just like a lamb from his mother.'

Paddy Roe

Why did the police do that?

'Well, I suppose they wanted to take them away to Missions.'

And there those children would have learned English and reading and writing?

'To read and write and all the sort of things they wanted to teach us. But my mother sent me away for good reason, to the desert with her young sister. So I grew up in the desert, Dampier Downs country.

'I learned making spears and boomerangs and shields and what the old people used to make, everything that the old people used to make. That was my education. And I used to hunt. Of course, that time I had to learn to hunt because we used to live off the land. No tea and sugar and flour and all these sort of things. No, we lived off the land. So that was a very handy thing, too, to me. I could hunt now, too, and make things. When I grew up in that country and got bigger, I came back to the station where my father and mother used to work. My father had a good boss there, too, because every time the boss knew the police were coming tomorrow, we got to go away today.

'He gave warning. He said, 'You better go'. They gave us stuff enough to stay [away] for a couple of days until the policemen went away again and we came back.'

The life Paddy came back to from his desert education was the typical life of a northwest stationhand, but in the white man's world he acquired another set of skills.

'When I learned to ride a horse, then I knew the game. I grew up a little bit bigger. We had sheep here, too, in this place, and my boss put me on the shearing, blade shearing in those

97

days. I used to shear the sheep with my boss. I used to do about four sheep a day for a start but I came good and [then] I used to do about a hundred sheep a day. I learned a lot of things on white man's side. Station work, cattle work, sheep work, shearing, putting up windmills, tanks, troughs, all concrete, everything.

'We always had Sunday off and I used to run the station when my boss used to go away for holidays back to his country in the Christmas time. I didn't know about reading and writing or anything but I knew the job right through.

'I had to take the boys out mustering. It was the rain time, Christmas time, and you've got to look after the sheep, put them out in the dry country. We used to do that, and windmills, fencing—we had to keep the fence always, and we did the sheepyards and cattleyards at the same time, you know, while the boss was away. When he came back everything was all ready for him to work.'

You weren't paid for doing that, were you?

'No, I never get paid. I wanted to get shirt and trousers, bread and meat, that's all. [It was only] one shirt and trousers a year so we had to put a lot of patches on them. White patch, black patch, all sorts of things.

'We never thought about any money those days, because we used to get a bit of money, when the boss used to be here we got a bit of money. We used to go into the pictures and we bought some cool drinks and that but we still brought two bob back from five shillings! We only spent three shillings. (Five shillings is roughly equivalent to fifty cents.)

'Films were all right. All right. We saw cowboys and all these things, fighting. We'd never seen a thing like that before.'

But a lot of Aboriginal people have seen things like that since then. Cinema, and later television, together with the growth of other contacts between Aboriginal and European society have made the survival of traditional culture much more difficult. So for Paddy, now retired from the white man's world of pastoral labour, the most important task is to try to pass on the stories, values and beliefs from his traditional society to younger people.

'We have to sit down with them and talk about it, or lay down with them, you know, at night-time and talk about it. We teach them more than the language but at the same time they're picking up the language, too, because they never had English, those Dreamtime people, they only had language. They're picking up the language, too, from the Dreamtime.'

Is it hard now to teach young Aboriginal people the knowledge of the past, the knowledge of the Dreamtime?

'Yes, a bit hard for us, because they got too many things to go to. They stop for corroborees, those sort of things, but other things, no.'

Do they want to know about the past, the young people?

'Yes, they like to know about the past, you know, from the olden times, but sometimes their friends come and, of course, they don't understand our ways. They might take them to pictures or basketball, or something else. We're losing our children; they don't take an interest. They think we're only telling them just a story.

'Any laws they had, the old people, that was all given to me too, the law and that. When I came to be a man they gave me everything. My culture. Now I'm still doing it. I'm teaching the young fellers the culture, making boomerangs, corroborees, initiation ceremonies, all these sort of things. It's all culture belonging to my people and we can't chuck it away.'

READING THE COUNTRY, *is a book Paddy created with the help of writer Stephen Muecke and artist Krim Bentiesak. It is a magical and spiritual as well as a physical way to look at landscape, its springs, rocks and waterholes.*

'I'm getting old now and I'm passing things over to my young generation. That's why I made the book, too, so they know the country.'

What does it mean exactly, when you talk about 'reading the country'?

'Reading the country, well, that's the waterholes and everything, finding food and all these sort of things. They've got to go from waterhole to waterhole.'

I can see from almost horizon to horizon but there are no trees, no sign of water out there. You tell me I could live out here.

'Yes, you can live here.'

Even in this immediate environment where I can see nothing of animal life or even any shelter or any water, there's food there, is there?

'You can't [see food or water] but they're here, they're here.'

Paddy, where we'd stopped to look at the bush at the side of the road, you picked up a beautiful plant. What do you call it?

'In the language, we call this one *mjourbi*. This is a very big thing to us in the medicine line, for babies. When the babies used to be born there was no medicine in those days. They used to put this in the coolamon, the wooden dish (like a cradle). They used to put it in and this plant smells all the time so the baby can't get cold or sick, because a new baby, new-born, must have *mjourbi*.'

How long has that been known about this plant?

'This one really is from the Dreamtime, too. It's not just new to us today. Sometimes old people got pain in their leg or chest or head, so they used to put this on, too. The old people used to heat it up in the fire to make it a bit more strong. Some sort of glue comes out of it when it's hot and it sticks.'

Paddy took me out to the land of his birth to show me the importance of its features—hills, trees and springs. Although he doesn't read or write, he reads the landscape like a map, charting its special features.

'We've got to go very close to see the trees up here. That's where I come from. That's my spirit. That's where I come from, my spirit place. My mother and father used to live in that country.'

So it's an important place to you.

'Yes, very important.'

Do you go back there many times?

'Yes, we go there nearly every week. I bring young fellers, my grandchildren all round the country. We ask the boss—we got to get permission to go through the fences, you know, but I go to station—because we want to go and have a look at the old country.'

We walked towards the special spring that Paddy had told me about, special because it was where he was born.

'Now, these springs belonged to the old people and when I was only a young feller and when these fellers—were finishing off, you know, were too old, they couldn't live any more, they passed all these things over to me. This is my country, I was born here, and the springs all belong to me now.'

Paddy, when you die, who does the spring belong to then?

'Well, I don't know, because I don't know which way my young fellers are looking today, because this is not their country, only mine. My daughter, she comes from Monari country.'

So those springs don't mean as much to them as they mean to you?

'Oh, well, the springs will be all right because they know the springs. The springs will be pretty safe with the grandsons because they have seen things. See, a cyclone can come out of these springs, too, so they're very important springs. I was in this country one time. I got out there and a cyclone came up. Next morning when we got up we saw the trees all broken down. So when we went back into town that morning I said to my people, "We're going to track this feller, this cyclone". There was one cyclone when we were standing outside Broome and he didn't want to let this other cyclone come—he picked him up and pushed him along. It's very hard to understand, but that's the way it goes. So I said to my people, "All right", I said, "We'll go and have a look". So we went to the Roebuck Plain turnoff to see where the cyclone came from. So, my daughters, grandsons, we all went with a 4-wheel drive right up to the turnoff and we saw the cyclone. He came out of one of these springs here now, straight through. That's why I say the springs will be pretty well safe when I die.'

You're saying then, Paddy, that as long as people know about the springs, the springs will be all right.

'Yes.'

What would happen if all the people went away and didn't care about the springs and didn't know about them? What would happen to the springs then?

'I think they'd finish, cover up. I'll show you one.'

To get to Paddy's spring we had to cross a few more fences but we found the spring in the corner of a paddock. It was, as Paddy said, just about all covered up. To me it was just a muddy waterhole. Cattle had trodden it and there was just a little clump of grasses there.
  You come to visit this spring. Is that important to the spring?

'Yes, it's important.'

Do you speak to the spring?

'Oh, I can, but as long as they get the smell of me, they know my smell.'

What about my smell? I'm a stranger.

'They can smell you, too, but you're here with me, so you must be a friend.'

If you decided to speak to the spring, what would you say to it?

'[I'd say] "I'm coming now, I'm a country man". [That's what] we say in our language. "Now", I say to myself, "I'm coming".'

What happens if we lose this spring?

'Well, if he wants to disappear on his own he can disappear. He can be all dry country, you won't see that wet, no more spring. He can cover himself.'

Would he come again in some other place?

'No, he won't come. But if the country man comes back again to this country, when he gets the smell of it again he can open up again.'

So it's not lost, even if he dies?

'He's not lost, but he's sorry if he is going to disappear. There's no smell of his people. That's the trouble.'

This country has changed a great deal since the white men came with cattle. Are the springs that you remember and your people remember disappearing?

'Oh, yes, just like that one, now. It's the cattle—too many cattle—tramping the place, you know, and the springs.'

If this spring disappears—gets covered up, as you say—what happens then? Does it never come again?

'If the real country man doesn't come back again; but if the country man comes back again [the springs] can open up, too.'

As long as people like you come around.

'Like me, yes. But I'm only one man left now for these springs and if I go I don't know what's going to happen.'

Alice Nannup

'I'll never be able to grasp why they take you from your parents. I suppose they thought they were doing good, but I don't know whether they were or not. They just didn't want half-castes to be mixed up with the full-bloods and they wanted to get them away on that account, I think.'

. . . .

Alice Nannup came from Roebourne near the north-west of Western Australia. She was born in 1912, the daughter of a European station owner and an Aboriginal mother. That relationship lasted for some years but when it ended Alice lost not only her parents and her home, but also her freedom. She was never to see either of her parents again.

The rest of her childhood was spent first in a Government institution and later in domestic service. Alice recalls her early childhood on a station near Roebourne before her parents' separation.

'One day at home on the station my father and mother said, "Oh, we'll go out for a drive in the sulky". We had an old horse called Kelly and when I heard mother and father talking I ran inside and said, "Mother", in Aboriginal. I said, "Not old Kelly, he'll bog, you know, and then we'll be stuck in the creek or somewhere". Father didn't like that. He said, "Listen here, child, when you speak in my presence, it's all English". So I just said, "Oh, sorry".

'I never called him Father in those days. His name was Tom and I called him Tommy. I had everything. I wanted for nothing. It was a really beautiful life. I had my own horse, I had a goat cart with my own goat called Tojo—he was the Japanese emperor in those days—and we called this bloke Tojo because he had a mean face.

'My father made me the cart and my sister and I used to cart wood for my mother. She was a great cook, a marvellous cook. She used to make rainbow cakes and sweet buns and bake bread in the camp oven. We never had a stove. But my mother got sick of being there. She wanted to go, to move on, so she and my father had a talk about it. I heard my father crying in the night—he didn't want to lose me. But wherever my mother went I had to go.'

When her parents separated Alice went to live with her mother on a reserve. As the child of a single parent, Alice now faced the risk, common to all part-European, part-Aboriginal children in the 1920s, of being scooped up by the Native Affairs Department and sent to a government settlement in the south of Western Australia at the orders of the Chief Protector of Aborigines, Mr A O Neville. At first, however, it looked as if Alice would escape this fate thanks to the Campbells, neighbours of her father. They offered to take Alice into their home. But before long the Campbells decided to retire from station life and go south. They offered to take Alice with them, with encouraging promises about her future.

'They spoke to our parents and said they would take us down to educate us because they were going away, they were retiring, you see. And when they were retiring they said, "Oh, we'll take them down with us and they can go to school down there". But the funniest part of it was—this is only just my thinking, you know, since I've grown up and thought it all over—they got Mr and Mrs Campbell to tell us that they were going to bring us down south, educate us and take us back home. But they only did this for a little while.

'When we came down on the boat, on the *Mindaroo*, I was sick all the way down with the seasickness. We couldn't eat and the boat had a balcony or whatever you call it and we used to sit out there. They never took us into the dining-room. We sat out there, wobbling, and with the water swaying, you know, and the food would just come up—we'd feed the fish.

'There was a great big box where they used to have these lifesaving jackets and we used to sit there and, of course, we used to talk in our own lingo those times, and we'd sit there and we'd cry for home. We used to say, "Oh, if we could only just go back home and be with our mother". It used to be heartbreaking.

'My father had a station. When he knew I was coming down he sold his property and came down with me, thinking that he'd be with me all the time, you know. But they barred him from seeing me. They didn't want him to have anything to do with me.

'It was just Aboriginal Affairs, you know. One Easter he rang them up and they said that he couldn't see me, so he sent me two boxes, one of Easter eggs and one of beautiful clothes—shoes and socks and beautiful dresses and everything I needed. Mrs Campbell said, "Oh, Alice, I had a phone call from Tommy today and he wanted to come and see you, have Easter with you, but we told him that he couldn't". And I said, "Why?". "Oh, well, that's what Mr Neville says. You're not allowed to see him any more."

'They never gave me a reason. He went back a very disappointed and a brokenhearted man, I suppose, because he loved me and I loved him, too. He may have written to me, you know, but I never ever got the letters. I couldn't write, but he wrote to me a couple of times and Mrs Campbell read the letters to me, but then I never ever heard from him any more. Many years later I had to go up to Wiluna and I met a lady who told me that my mother had passed away, and my sister, and my father. So I never thought more about it. That was just terrible. I thought, "Oh, well, I'll never see them again". And in Geraldton here I met a girl named Gertrude.

Gertie told me that my father had saved eighteen sovereigns for me and said, "I'll never give up. If it's the last thing I do, I'll go back down south and I'll go until I find her." And he had a calico bag and he said, "I've got this—eighteen sovereigns. They're all for her, when I meet her." And, of course, that didn't eventuate because there was foul play. They found my Dad dead in his hut and the sovereigns were gone. So I never saw him or anything else. And in his will he left me £400 and I never even received that.'

Alice's future was now in the hands of the Campbells and the Native Affairs Department. This was the body presided over by the Chief Protector of Aborigines, Mr A O Neville, a man with total control over their destiny. It was Mr Neville who decided what would happen to Alice despite the Campbells' pledge to her parents.

'Mr and Mrs Campbell said, "We'll take the kids down, educate them and we'll bring them back home". But we never ever got back. And the schools closed and, of course, we had to come to Mogumber, and this was the cunning way they did it, I think.

'When they took us to the Department they spoke to us and Mr Neville did. Then they sent us outside and they had a chat on their own, and that's where we ended up, in Mogumber. That's what caused me to be so bitter about it all. When we were shoved into the Mission, well, that was the end of everything, you know. I just gave up all hope.'

Alice Nannup was then thirteen.

'In 1925 we went to Mogumber, three of us kids. The train was a bit late that night and when we got to Mogumber we were just taken into the dormitory. Everybody else was in bed and we woke up in the morning to find little black faces all over the place. I'd never seen anything like it in my life and I was so worried and upset. Some of them were friendly, some of them were hostile, some of them wanted fights. The first thing they asked you was where you came from, and if you said, north, the nor'west girls would take you under their wings and the sou'westers would stick on one side with the nor'westers on the other. Then we had to go to school. We got up in the morning, washed, dressed, and went up to breakfast. We had semolina and a piece of bread and dripping, with black tea with saccharine in it or molasses or something. Anyway, that was our breakfast and it was terrible. And the vessels we had to drink out of, oh, dear, dear! At tea time you'd get bread and dripping and jam, just a scrape of jam. That was all you had for tea and then this gruel and a piece of bread and fat for breakfast, that's all you had. Christmas time they used to make puddings and things like that. It might have been a little better than the ordinary meals we had. Other than that it was just one thing the whole time.

There is a happy land far, far away
Where we get bread and scrape three times a day
Bread and butter we never see,
No sugar in our tea
While we are gradually starving away.

'That's the song we used to sing often, especially when we were feeling hungry.'

. . . .

Apart from the daily routine there was a social life of sorts: dances at weekends and sport in the afternoons. But for the most part, Moore River offered a certain level of schooling and after that just preparation for work beyond the compound gates. Alice recalls that the schooling didn't count for much.

'They didn't want to give us a real education. Mr Neville

said one day, "As long as they can count money and write their name, that is all they need". What sort of an education is that? I didn't know much when I left the school. I knew how to read Dolly and Ben and whatever you call it—Ben and Dora, or Dick and Dora, or whatever it was, and write my name. All I got up to was the Third Grade and then I had to go out and work.

'They had to make clothes for the Forest River Mission and they needed girls, so they took me out of school. They took about four of us out of school and took us down to the sewing room where all the girls had machines and sewing. Well, we *did* have to work. They had a lady there doing the cutting out, and we had to get these clothes done. They had Singer machines and one Jones and that was the Number One machine, you know. So I set a goal one day. I said, "I'll make as many shirts as I can", and I knocked out sixteen shirts in one day. So the sewing mistress said to me, "You broke the record today", and I said, "Yeah?" and she said, "You've got to keep that up". I said, "Oh, I don't know, I mightn't be able to do it next time". So we had to work on pants then, on trousers, dungarees, and I did eight pairs of pants, trousers, in one day. So the Jones machine was handed to me. I took it over. But we had to work, I tell you. And you know what we used to get paid every Saturday morning? A bar of chocolate. No money, we never saw money. We thought we were just marvellous—getting paid, you know. Chocolates!

'At Christmas time we were allowed to have a piece of material and we had to make our own choice of the material we wanted and make it the way we wanted it. I chose this beautiful, plaid sort of a thing it was and I made myself a dress. So when we were going to church I wore this beautiful frock and all the boys on the other side, all ready to go to church, they whistled and said, "Oooh, look at the butterfly". They called me the butterfly! Oh, dear, I just went back inside and waited for the other girls to come out and then we all went to church.'

. . . .

There were some compensations. Moore River lay in pleasant, open countryside and there was a river with deep pools, pleasures worth breaking some of the rules for.

'If we wanted to go for a swim in the afternoons—the kitchen girls would go—we'd ask Mr G, I'll call him, if we could go for a swim, and he'd say "Oh, yes, you can go". One day he said, "I'm going away today, girls, but" he said, "I don't want you to leave the house". I said, "All right", because I had more responsibility than Eva did. When the girls had finished their work they came over to the fence and said, "You coming for a swim?" and I said, "No, we're not allowed to go today, Mr G said we weren't to go". They said, "Oh, come on, we'll be back before he gets back". You know, you're easily led, aren't you? So I said, "Oh, well, come on Eva, we'll go". So we went. Instead of hiding the key I took it with me, locked the house up and off we went, down to the river. We had no time, no watches or anything like that; we used to watch the sun. So, anyway, we were having a good old swim there and I said, "Oh, I think it's about time we took off because we don't know when Mr G will be back. He might be back now." They said, "All right, we'll go".

'We had to go across a great big log over this dirty-looking pool. Anyway, when we picked up our clothes, I picked up my frock and I had a safety pin on the belt with the key on it. And as we were walking back over this log I shook my frock over the pool. In went the key, down into the murky pool. Eva looked back and said, "What's the matter?" and I said "Oh, no! The key", and she said, "How are we going to get it out? We'll never find it." The other girls were there, and one said, "Oh, I think I know where it is, I heard it plop down there". So she got into the pool and dived down. In the meantime, from nowhere came this tracker, Ginger his name was, and he went off his brain and said, "What are you girls doing here? You're not allowed here, you know that." He said, "You come straight to the office". I said, "Look, Ginger, I lost the key from the house". He said "Where?" and I said, "Down there". "Well, you stand there", he said. So I walked to the log and I said. "Straight down there, Ginger". He walked right around so that he wouldn't stir the water up and he mumbled something in his language. Down he went and he was down there for a few mintues and he came up. Down he went again [then] he came up with the key. "Oh, thank you, Ginger, thank you!" I said. "That doesn't help you", he said, "you're coming to the office just the same". We all went over the log and I said, "Ginger, you're not going to take us to the office, are you?" He said, "Yeah, you're not allowed to go anywhere you're not allowed to go". So I thought, now what am I going to do? We had a wild turkey a few days before and it was cooked and everything, and I said to him, "Ginger," I said, "if I give you some *munga* you won't take me to the office?" He was just as hungry as we were, you see. And he said, "What sort of *munga*?". I said, "Turkey", and he said "Yeah, but I want bread with it, too". I said, "Yeah, I'll give you bread". He said, "All right, I won't take you to the office". He followed us straight to the house and I opened the door and said, "Eva, get in there and get that turkey and half a loaf of bread". I kept on talking to him, you know, keeping sweet with him, and gave it to him and he went off and we didn't get reported. We were lucky that day! I reckon we were lucky.

'The first job I had, I didn't know where I was going or what I was doing. They never even told me where I was going. When I got there this tall gentleman came to me and he said,

"You're Alice Nannup?" and I said, "Yes". He said, "Come along with me", and lo and behold it was to a Police Station. Now fancy that! When I got to the living quarters there was an invalid lady and she was a Roman Catholic. She said to me, "What religion are you?". I said, "Church of England", and she said, "I asked for a Catholic girl". She was a little bit abrupt. "And how old are you?" I said, "Sixteen". She said, "I wanted a woman". I said, "I'll do all I can for you, I'll do my best". And she said, "Yes, and perhaps you'll turn Catholic, too, one day", and I said "No". She wasn't happy about that, but I had to get her set up—she had Holy Communion, you know— and Constable Larsen had to go out all day so I had to take 'phone calls and I'm no scholar, you know, I didn't know how to do things. But I used to write them down best I could. They were good to me. She had rheumatoid arthritis and she taught me a lot because she taught me how to cook and she taught me how to dressmake, because she was a seamstress herself. She was a very tall lady and she couldn't wear her dresses any more. I used to unpick the skirts and make dresses out of them for me, beautiful they were. I dressed myself up nicely with all the beautiful dresses she had.'

When Mrs Larsen died Alice found work on a farm, became ill, and while recovering was offered a job with Mr A O Neville, the man who'd arranged for her to go to Moore River back in 1925.

'I was thrilled. I never thought about him taking me away from my home or anything like that, you know. I thought, Oh, working for the Chief Protector, that's a great honour. Wouldn't you, if you were a girl like me? Anyway, I went out there on the tram and they met me. It was different to what Mrs Larsen was—they were just ordinary people. But you had to wear a cap and apron and uniform. They were very party-going, bridge, bridge, bridge—two or three times a week, you know—and I had to do the cooking and everything. Because I was working for the Chief Protector I got more wages that I did in any other place. I was getting 15/- a week and my keep. He was very nice, very fatherly. He had his office and his room—we had a long building and there was the laundry, and my room, and Mr Neville's room. He lived in the house with his wife and family, but if he wanted to be quiet he'd go into his little room. I used to sleep on the back verandah on hot nights, but if it was cool I'd sleep in the room. So, anyway, I went up to the room this night and I got undressed and got into bed and there was a lump, a distinct lump under the bed. I pressed down and that lump moved: there was a man in my room! I just ran out of the room screaming and Mr Neville came around. He had a revolver in his hand and "In the Queen's name", he said, "answer me or I'll fire". Of course, this man was sliding down the steep hill, and he fired a shot and the man just slid down and lay there for a minute. He was out for stealing. I said, "I'm not sleeping here", so Mr Neville said, "Come round there, my child, and we'll find you a bed around there". And I slept around in the sleep-out with them all, you know. He was really good like that. He was really fatherly. They were very good entertainers. They liked bridge. I'd have to sit up at 11 o'clock at night waiting to serve supper and that's where I used to learn to write. I'd buy a pad and I'd sit there and I'd get whatever I saw and I'd write and write, to test my hand so I could write. Because I never had any education, you see, I was only in Grade 3 when I left.'

For the next few years Alice continued to do domestic work on stations and farms and later she settled in Geraldton, where she still lives, but a long way south of her old home in Roebourne in the north-west. At Moore River she and her friends could only talk about how wonderful it would be to see family and friends again.

'Some friends came from Derby. There was a beautiful girl named Alice—we were both Alices—and we used to sit and talk and she said, "I'd love to go back home," she said, "but how am I going to get back home?" You see, we were so dumb. We could have gone to work and saved money and gone back home, you know, but we didn't think of that. I did it after forty-two years, I went back home, I could have done it before I even got married, you know.'

When she did go home she found only a few of her people.

'My mother's sister was the only living auntie I had. I went there one morning, at about half-past seven, to my auntie's little place. They were getting ready for breakfast. I got down there and I went and got out of the car and I walked over to them and they were just getting breakfast. She wasn't well, but my Uncle Bill was cooking breakfast. I went to the door and knocked and they looked, and I said, "Good morning". They said, "Good morning". I said, "Do you know who I am?" and they said, "No". I said, "You don't?". "No, we don't know you". I was just going to say something else and, I don't know, I just laughed, and my Uncle Bill said, "It's not Alice, is it?" and I said, "That's me!" Well look, the game was on. There were tears and laughter and everything, you know—they couldn't believe it, because I was only a little girl when I left home.'

Margaret Colbung

'Like my parents and my grandparents said, if we're going to get anywhere and be recognised as Aboriginal people and set out to achieve something, we have to have some education, and I think from there on I just went along that line.'

. . . .

For Margaret Colbung, as for many Aboriginal children in the 1950s, getting something for themselves out of the education system wasn't easy. Margaret's family lived in, or rather on, the edge of town, the town of Narrogin, a typical wheat and sheep country centre in the Great Southern District of Western Australia.

Although her parents and her grandparents had tried for a long time to get a better deal for Aboriginal people in the district Margaret recalls that working and living conditions were not easy when she was a child.

'My father used to be a seasonal worker. He used to get jobs on farms shearing or clearing or seeding or hay-carting, things like that, and we used to go out onto the farms and live and we used to have temporary accommodation, which was usually made up of a couple of tents and you'd have a bough shed or, if you could find the material, you'd have a structure built. But there were no permanent things because they could be pulled down when you went back into town again.

'[There] were really bad winters. Sometimes, if the owners of the farms were good people, they'd say, "Okay, you can use the shearing shed", or they might have a shed that they weren't using that you could move into. Otherwise it was very cold.'

One thing I imagine might have been a problem would have been trying to do homework, especially if you were sometimes in temporary quarters.

'That was always a problem. We didn't have any electricity and we'd learned to adapt ourselves to the situation. Either we'd find time during the course of the day to do our homework or we'd fit it in during one period or one lesson at school, or, if we were travelling on the bus, do it either going home or coming in in the morning. But that always was a problem.'

Supposing because of those circumstances you couldn't always get your homework in on time, what was the attitude of teachers towards that situation?

'We'd have to be punished regardless of what our excuses [were]. If we said that we couldn't do it because of light or anything, that wasn't taken into account. If we didn't have our homework we were punished.'

Did you ever try to explain that sort of problem to teachers?

'Most times . . . but in the end you got so you made sure your homework was there, because it's not very nice being singled out in a classroom of thirty or forty children.'

What sort of effect did that have on your education, the fact that your father was working out of town like that?

'The whole family would go out of town. We'd move out and live with them and we'd have to catch a bus in to school when the bus came past and catch it home in the afternoon, but [I have] really very vivid memories of being sick every time because I used to get travelling sickness a lot, especially travelling in to school and travelling home in the afternoon. I was really glad when Dad had finished his seasonal work and moved into

117

town. Then, later on, towards the end of the primary school years, we went to high school and he got a permanent job on the railways, so we were sort of permanently based in town.

'The other thing is that the Aboriginal children weren't allowed to sit in the front of the bus. When we got on the bus there were four seats, two on each side of the aisle, that were just there specially for the Aboriginal children, and in the morning the kids used to put their school bags in the aisleway and we used to have to battle to get from the front of the bus down to the back of the bus, and when you'd get off the same thing would happen again, and that was truly an experience in itself, just getting an education.

'Because of the attitude of the people that were in the school, or the attitude of the communities or the society at that particular time towards Aboriginal people, it was really very hard just to maintain some sort of position within the school. That showed itself in the way that the teachers actually treated the children. I can remember sitting in the classroom and most times we always had to sit down the back. All the time I was at school, during those early years at primary school, that was where I always sat, down the back of the classroom. Needless to say I wasn't very happy about going to school at that time, because once you were out in the playground you were treated like some sort of a leper. Kids didn't want to know you or they didn't want to have you involved with their games, so all the Aboriginal kids used to get in their little groups all around the school yards and things like that.

'It was worse for girls because I think at that particular time [most] girls were timid. A couple of the girls, and my sister in particular, were really fiery about it and if they felt we were being mistreated in any way there used to be huge fights in the grounds. But I can always remember my uncle [a bigger boy] who, if he saw something being done to an Aboriginal child at school, would always stick up for them. One day there was this big huge fight around the back of the school. The teachers knew about it but they didn't do anything. But the kids said, "Okay, we'll settle this around the back", and all of the school practically was at this fight. There was a big ring and just two [of them], my uncle and another boy, and they just let them go, just a bare fist fight. I can remember that one, and that all started over just one of the children calling names to one of the Aboriginal children.

'Some of the teachers were supportive, but I expect they could only go so far, that being the environment, because they could possibly get offside, I suppose, with the education system. The Aboriginal children resented that as well because even though you had one or two teachers that were supportive to the Aboriginal children there wasn't much they could do, so I suppose that's where a lot of resentment came about, too, at school. That followed me all the way through high school until the time I left.'

You've obviously survived education through all this. How do you think you did that?

'I did it because of the insistence of my parents, because they said that that's the only way that we as an Aboriginal race of people were going to survive. To do that we had to be educated to learn the white man's system. But there was also another turning point in that, and what really got my back up about the whole issue was that I particularly wanted to do a course during high school and not to just sort of go through and say, well, I've been to high school and received the Higher School Certificate. I'd made approaches to the headmistress at the high school at that particular time, and she informed me that, even though she thought that I had the potential to be able to do a professional course, she didn't think that I'd be able to stay the distance, and that it wasn't my fault, it was my parents' fault, because they didn't have enough little grey cells in the brains to be able to do that. Well, that really got my back up so I said, "Okay, if that's how you're going to feel about this whole thing, and not give any encouragement", and I went to the Native Welfare Officer, as it was at that time, and said, "Look, you do something about my education. You either send me away or do something about that so I can get some sort of education."

'I'd received the Daisy Bates Memorial Prize, I think it was, and through that had got some further recognition and I got sent away. Actually they sent me away to school in Perth to do a year or so, and when I did get my Junior Certificate I made sure that the headmistress of that school received a copy of it and another little letter to go with it. So I think that's one of the things that pushed me to make sure that I did get some sort of education.'

Today, Margaret Colbung is the administrator of a Community Aboriginal Health Centre in the coastal town of Geraldton. When she left high school she trained to be a nurse:

'Nursing's one of those things where you're doing for other people and when they're within institutions they have their laws and the people who use them abide by those laws, including the nursing staff, so [I didn't have] many setbacks. You might have had your few little hassles from patients who used to say, "Well, I don't want an Aboriginal black person touching me or doing this thing or the other". But if you happen to be the only person on duty, and there weren't other people around to do their beck and call, they just had to make do with what was there.'

Did you ever find yourself having to stand up for yourself as a person when that happened?

120

'Only on one occasion and just for peace at that time I chose not to deal with it and left it up to the hospital administration. But that was in particular to a very uptight non-Aboriginal person.'

Did you find yourself having to bite your tongue sometimes¿

'Very much so. You learn a lot of patience, I think, and understanding with nursing, but sometimes it gets a little bit beyond you.'

Looking back on your childhood, do you feel any bitterness or resentment¿

'If you'd asked me this question say about ten or fifteen years ago I'd have said I resented it, very much so, and I suppose to some degree that sort of resentment's still there. But since that time I've come to understand that it's a two-way thing. Aboriginal people have always had to be understanding and tolerant of white people. Now [the boot's] on the other foot as far as I'm concerned. There has to be that leeway, there has to be that ability for the white people to now come around and understand the Aboriginal way of life and the culture that exists as well. I think that now's the time and it's not too late—it's never too late—for white people to have a look at where this whole thing is going. Because we're not going to disappear. I mean, we're not going to move off out of this country at all. We're going to be here, and up until now it's always been the Aboriginal person who's had to adjust, who's had to cope with society as it is. Now, I think that there has to be that little leeway given as well, that the white people have to come to the party.'